Vanessa's Kitchen

Pure Food Joy!

Vanessa Argentieri

To my Mother, Lynne
an amazing cook
and teacher.

To my friend Jamie,
the inspiration for
this book and to all
of my loved ones who
supported me on
this endeavor.

Table of Contents

Introduction

Welcome, friends, to my kitchen. I am so happy that you have joined me!

My kitchen is a place where love, laughter, and delicious food flows. It is a hearth where family and friends gather to taste, sip and indulge in pure food creations.

Over the years I've worked to perfect my favorite pure food recipes and now I'm ready to share them in this inviting book for everyone to enjoy! These recipes are personal favorites; a conglomeration of cuisines and a world of taste. Through extensive experimentation, sampling and research, I made each dish delicious and nutritious. This book is a source of yummy recipes, pure food shopping strategies, pantry essentials, nourishing advice, better baking tips and Holiday delights.

Each food chapter unfolds with seasonal ingredients from spring to winter, a rhythm which benefits the family budget and local farmers. The *Ingredient Index* (pg 137) will help you match the perfect recipe with the food items you have on hand or which are on sale in the store. Using this index can help to prevent waste and save money. The *Subject Index* (pg 131) will direct you quickly to the perfect dish for every meal, situation and diet. This index lists recipes that are slow-cooker friendly, quick-cooking dishes and lunch box bites, plus recipes for vegan, vegetarian, paleo, gluten free and raw diets.

I highly respect that we each have unique needs in terms of nutrition and lifestyle. Therefore I strive to accommodate the taste and traditions of everyone in a healthy way. My hope is that there will be happy faces and healthy bodies for your whole family through the quality foods that are prepared each day! ℘

About the Author

Culinary arts and agriculture have always been my passion; a gift that's naturally inherited from my mother and grandmothers. I began writing and collecting recipes at the age of 8. I've gone from mud pies to bake sales, winning cooking contests and cooking for many friends. When it came time for college, I was a torn between studying culinary arts or agriculture. I ended up going the agriculture route, knowing I could always prepare yummy food for my family and friends.

During my youth, farming was always a dream of mine. As a student of agriculture I was excited to get my hands in the dirt. As my prescribed course load unraveled, my romantic notion of farming was snuffed. I witnessed how farming was about mass feeding rather than farming for food quality and flavor. I learned about cloning of animals and genetic modification of plants; practices that are taxing to authentic plant and animal species as well as taxing to our bodies and environment.

As a result, I soon gained great appreciation for our food producers who practice sustainable and organic farming methods. These methods help to preserve authentic plant and animal species along with our natural resources so that they are clean and usable for our children and beyond.

I wasn't given the opportunity to become an organic or sustainable farmer. Instead, by pursuing my passion in cooking and nutrition I found a way to support that desire by creating and sharing delicious pure food recipes and tips with my family and friends. I define pure food as food that is grown using natural and organic methods. Food that is not genetically modified (GMO) and foods that are minimally processed, minimally refined and free of toxic additives such as MSG, artificial ingredients and other chemical residues.

When I began raising my own children, proper nourishment for their growing bodies became a big factor in parenting. These influences inspired me to get into the "dirt" on food ingredients and nutrition. I became determined to enhance my favorite recipes by preparing them with the healthiest ingredients. Delicious, pure food became my passion for my family meals. My fellow mommy friends soon saw me as a source of helpful information and asked me to write down my recipes so they could help their families enjoy pure food as well. The result is this book, which is filled with some of my favorite pure food recipes and tips. ❧

Pantry Preparation

Make a new habit of shopping for and stocking pure foods so that nutritious snacks and meals are easy to prepare each day. This chapter offers advice on how to move away from refined and processed foods and over to a pure food kitchen.

My Definition of Pure Foods - Foods grown using natural and organic methods, not genetically modified (non-GMO) and minimally processed, minimally refined and free of toxic additives such as MSG, artificial ingredients and other chemical residues. ✍

Steps for Successful Pure Food Shopping and Meal Preparation:

1. Start your weekly meal planning with the seasonal, fresh, local and organic produce. Typically the seasonal fresh produce is the produce that is on sale in the market or can be found in the co-op box from the local CSA (community supported agriculture).

2. Search and select recipes from the *Ingredient Index* (pg 137) that use the seasonal, fresh produce items on hand. Once you've selected your recipe or recipes, check the *Suggested Pairings* offered with each recipe to help make your weekly meals come together. For efficiency, choose recipes that ask for ingredients that match what is already on hand in your pantry, fridge and freezer or what is on sale at the store. Then create a shopping list reflecting items that are needed to complete each recipe.

3. Shop and Stock-up on pure food ingredients for daily recipe success. *Pure Food Essentials* (pg 14) are the building blocks for all the healthy meals that I create. To save money I stock up on them when they are on sale; they will never go to waste. When shopping, be sure to check the labels on packaged products. Avoid purchasing products that have unhealthy, vague or unknown ingredients.

4. Plan and Prepare weekly meals ahead of time. I like to prepare *Sensational Salads* (pg 75) and/or *Superb Soups* (pg 67) at the beginning of the week so they are on hand when the days are rushed. I pair these with *Simple Proteins* (pg 33) for fast meals. I also will prepare one or two *Fabulous Feast* (pg 87) recipes so the leftovers can be enjoyed for several days following.

Shopping carts are the vehicles to healthy eating.

Pure Food Essentials

Having the necessary, quality ingredients on hand makes pure food cooking a natural success.

I strive to purchase organic/clean foods and always try to serve a variety of colorful foods each day. The items I have specified as "organic" are typically the most contaminated when produced conventionally. Therefore I suggest purchasing them only in organic form to avoid chemical toxins.

Fresh and Frozen Foods

These ingredients are the foundation for healthy meals. The *Pantry Essentials* (pg 7) and *Spices and Seasonings* (pg 10) will help to make all dishes complete.

Staple veggies/fruits: Organic carrots, onions and bananas. These produce items are always on hand in my kitchen because they are always available, affordable and end up in many of my dishes.

Ripened (yellow with brown spots) bananas make a great snack when slathered with nut butter on top. I like to freeze very ripe bananas for future smoothies and baked goods. Carrots are an easy crunchy snack and also add nourishment to many savory and sweet dishes.

Seasonal leaves/greens: Organic spinach, peas, organic arugula, asparagus, organic chard, organic lettuce, organic green beans, fresh herbs, broccoli, organic kale, organic mustard greens and more.

Seasonal root veggies: Yams, sweet potatoes, organic beets, parsnips, turnips and organic potatoes.

Other seasonal veggies: Cabbages, cauliflower, celery, eggplant, organic cucumbers, organic celery, Belgium endive, kohlrabi, organic zucchini, summer squash, organic beans, organic bell peppers, chilis, Brussel sprouts and winter squash.

Seasonal fruits: Avocado, pineapple, oranges, lemons, melon, mango, kiwi, organic berries, organic peaches, organic apricot, cherries, papaya, persimmon, organic nectarines, organic tomatoes, organic grapes, organic plums, organic pears, organic apples, figs, pomegranate and grapefruit.

Dairy: Organic butter, organic milk, quality cheeses, organic plain whole milk yogurt and/or sour cream and heavy cream.

Milk: Suitable cow's milk alternatives are almond milk, coconut and goat's milk.

Naturally raised eggs: Free range, local, farm raised and organic are best.

Juices: Orange juice (not from concentrate), organic apple, berry and veggie juice. I like to purchase juices that are less than 28 grams of sugar per serving.

Natural and organic meats: Naturally raised and organic meats are the best for our bodies and our planet. Natural meats from local farmers are the optimum choice.

Quality fish and seafood: Typically wild caught and northern pacific are the best choice.

Fresh garlic

Fresh ginger

Fresh herbs: Dill, parsley, basil, chives, cilantro, sage, mint, thyme and rosemary. Use what is available depending on the season.

Sauces and condiments: Organic ketchup, yellow mustard, Dijon or whole grain mustard, organic mayonnaise and hot sauce.

Pickles, krauts, and peppers: Natural or organic pickles, naturally fermented "raw" sauerkraut (see pg 26), hot peppers and roasted red peppers. ❧

Pantry Essentials

Keep your pantry stocked with these ingredients, and healthy, delicious recipes will come together with ease.

Raw apple cider vinegar: "Raw" means it is unfiltered and still contains the naturally occurring probiotics or "mother". Apple cider vinegar is a wonderful natural cleanser for our bodies and our homes.

Balsamic vinegars: Balsamic vinegar is a great source of antioxidants. I keep two types on hand. The first is a *premium balsamic vinegar*, one that is aged over 18 years, and is very smooth, perfect for a simple dressing over veggies, fruits and cheeses. The second is a younger, less expensive *basic balsamic vinegar*. I use this for cooking veggies and meats and making salad dressings.

Premium extra virgin olive oil: To ensure quality, always purchase First Cold Pressed organic olive oil. Look for an olive oil that has a greenish hue and a rich flavor. Inexpensive olive oils typically are a blend of vegetable oils and are yellow in color.

Virgin coconut oil: A tropical treasure that has an abundance of healthy, healing properties. Coconut oil can help boost immunity, act as a natural antiseptic and heal damaged tissue. Coconut oil is wonderful for high heat cooking. It also adds amazing flavor and texture to baked goods, and is great for popping corn (see pg 58) Enjoy it as a raw spread instead of butter or nut butter. Make your own delicious ***Coco-nut Spread***. To do so, simply mix together equal parts of coconut oil, nut or seed butter and raw honey. Add in 1-2 Tbs. unsweetened cocoa powder and pure almond extract. This spread is perfect for crepes and sprouted bread or enjoyed with a spoon.

Ghee: Ghee is clarified butter, which is the butter's fat without the dairy proteins. It is perfect for high heat cooking; a substitute for butter, olive oil and coconut oil.

Natural nut and seed butters: Peanut, tahini, cashew, sunflower and almond butter.

Toasty nuts and seeds: (see pg 15 & 16) Almonds, pecans, sunflower, pumpkin, sesame and walnuts. I like to have at least two of these on hand for my pure food recipe needs. For super nutritious nuts and seeds I like to soak, sprout and dehydrate them (see pg.15). They are the perfect snack and a gluten-free base for baked goods. They are also crunchy additions to many savory dishes.

Dried fruits: Dried fruits have been consumed for over 5,000 years. They are one of civilizations first sources of sugar. Many of the recipes in this book will use these healthy bites to sweeten dishes naturally. Organic raisins, organic apricots, dates, figs and naturally sweetened cranberries are the ones that I use the most. I pack them in lunches instead of packaged "fruit snacks".

Dried, flaked unsweetened coconut: A healthy base for baking and making raw fruit truffles. See recipes on pg 112. Refer to pg 15 for a tip on how to toast coconut.

Whole grain spelt flour or organic whole wheat flour: I prefer baking with whole grain spelt flour because it is lighter and has less gluten than whole wheat flour, but both are healthy flour choices.

Corn flour: I use this for gluten-free fruit cobbler, crepes, corn bread and savory dishes, too.

Corn grits (aka polenta): A lovely substitute for pasta. See recipes for *Chili N' Grits* on pg 52 and *Polenta Lasagna* on page pg 88.

Organic all-purpose flour

Tapioca flour and arrowroot powder: Both of these are gluten-free thickening agents that make a great substitute for corn starch. I use them for thickening gravies and custards as well as preparing gluten-free baked goods.

Almond flour: Perfect for gluten-free baking and raw food bites

Unsweetened cocoa powder: Preferably fair trade or organic.

Whole grains: Organic oats, quinoa, brown rice, wild rice, millet, and more.

Organic chicken, veggie and beef broths: (see recipes on pg 29 and 30)

Organic canned tomatoes: Diced tomatoes, tomato paste, crushed tomatoes, sauce and salsas.

Organic canned and dried legumes: Garbanzo, kidney, black, pinto, great northern, navy and lentils are the types that I recommend. I try to stock up on them when they are on sale or cook my own at home and store them in the freezer (see pg 17)

Organic whole fruit preserves: Stock up on jars of apricot, blackberry, strawberry and more when on sale at the store. I like to use these natural sweeteners for baking, making glazes and adding to smoothies.

Coconut milk: A nourishing, vegan alternative for creamed sauces and baked goods.

Natural BBQ sauce: Always be sure it is made with pure cane sugar and honey, not corn syrup and MSG.

Tamari or liquid aminos: These are the healthiest options for "soy sauce".

Raw honey: Nature's medicine and a natural source of vitamins and minerals. I keep two types on hand, the thick type for frostings and spreads and a liquid type for dressings and dips. Take note, most commercial honeys in the market have been heated through pasteurization, therefore destroying the nutrients in the honey. Always choose "raw", "local" and or "unfiltered".

Pure maple syrup: Another great natural sweetener that adds depth of flavor to sweets, breakfast treats and savory dishes too. Maple syrup will not harden when chilled, therefore it is an ideal sweetener for smoothies. Be sure to buy "pure" to avoid added refined sugars.

Agave nectar: An alternative to maple syrup that is good for smoothies, shakes and granolas.

Coconut sugar: Derived from the coconut blossom, one of the most sustainable, pure sugars in the market. It is brownish in color and can be used as a substitute for pure cane and brown sugar.

Natural brown sugar also known as "sucanat": This dehydrated pure cane sugar is the least refined sugar. It can be found in most markets by the natural sugars. It is a light brown color because the sugar still contains its natural molasses content. Most common brown sugar found in the market is a refined white sugar with molasses added in.

Organic turbinado sugar and or organic pure cane sugar: These two types of sugar are essentially the same but Turbinado, aka "raw sugar", has a larger crystal.

Organic molasses: Molasses offers sweet nourishment in cakes, cookies, breads and sauces. Molasses is the source of nutrients in the sugar cane plant, and the byproduct of refining sugar cane. Be sure to purchase it organically to avoid any impurities.

Chocolate: When shopping for chocolate, try to choose organic or fair trade, semisweet or bittersweet. Read the label to be sure there are only a few ingredients. It should read "unsweetened chocolate, cocoa butter, pure cane sugar, and vanilla". Most chocolate contains "soy lecithin" which is a highly processed food binder and smoother. There are several brands on the market that do not have this ingredient.

Pure vanilla extract
Pure almond extract
Pure anise extract
Aluminum free baking powder
Baking Soda
Organic/Fair trade coffee and teas

Spices, Seasonings and Dried Herbs

Cooking with fresh spices and dried herbs provides the most flavorful dishes. To ensure fresh flavor and prevent waste, I keep a standard stash of spices, seasoning and dried herbs that can be incorporated in all of the dishes I prepare. Listed below are the standard spices, seasonings and dried herbs that can be used in so many ways throughout my whole recipe collection.

Sea salt, both fine and course ground
Ground black pepper
Garlic powder
Ground cinnamon
Oregano
Thyme
Rosemary
Basil
Bay leaves
Ground cumin
Ground red pepper (cayenne or other favorite type of chili pepper)
Red Pepper flakes

Chili powder
Curry powder (a blend of turmeric and other healthy spices)
Sweet paprika
Smoked paprika
Ground ginger
Whole nutmeg with grater
Ground allspice
Cloves (ground and whole)
Ground cardamom
Fennel Seeds
Turmeric

Wines and Liquors for Enhanced Flavors

Wines and liquors have a way of accentuating the natural flavor of foods. Cooking with wine and liquor has been a tradition for centuries. Wines and liquors are typically the byproducts of fermented fruits, grain and veggies. The fermentation of foods was the first means of food preservation, prior to refrigeration methods. The premium liquors on hand in my pantry add amazing flavor to many special occasion dishes.

Dry red wine: Perfect flavor booster for many beef and lamb dishes. Save the unfinished bottle for the next marinade, sauce or stew.

Dry white wine: A wonderful compliment to many fish, chicken, seafood dishes, sauces and soups. Save the unfinished bottle of Chardonnay or Sauvignon Blanc to enhance the flavor of many dishes.

Brandy: Perfect for savory sauces, fruit desserts and whipped creams.

Cognac and orange liquor blend: Such as Grand Marnier or Cointreau. The perfect addition to holiday desserts and fruit salads.

Bourbon: Perfect for chocolate desserts and whipped creams, too.

Chambord: Great flavor enhancement for your holiday fruit salads.

Dark rum: Choose a quality spiced rum, perfect for holiday desserts.

Kitchen Equipment

A properly equipped kitchen makes preparing food easy. These are the items that I like to have handy for all my culinary needs.

Pans and Baking Dishes:

Three seasoned cast iron skillets
   (see pg 12)
One or two large, heavy-bottomed
   sauté pans
One large griddle for pancakes, etc.
Small, medium and large sauce pans
   with lids
One large stock pot
One medium stock pot
Vegetable steamer basket that fits in
   the stock pots
One or two roasting pans
One or two medium sized dutch ovens
   (a pot that can go in the oven and
   on the stove)

Two 13x9 inch glass baking dishes
Two 11x7 or 8x8 glass baking dishes
Two full size jelly roll pans
   (sheet pan with sides)
Two cookie sheets
Two loaf pans
One 6-inch pie plate
Two 9-inch pie plates
Six 1 cup ramekins
Two 8-inch cake pans
Two 9-inch cake pans
One 8-inch spring form pan
One 10-inch tart pan
One or two 12-cup muffin pans
One mini muffin pan

Tools:

Immersion blender
Standard sized food processor with
   shredding attachment
Electric mixer
Slow cooker
Measuring cups
Measuring spoons
Cheese grater
Lemon zester
Quality knife set
One meat cutting board (ideally
   dishwasher safe for sterilization)

One fruit and veggie cutting board
One bread and cheese cutting board
Large wire whisk
Metal spatulas
Rubber spatulas
Pastry cutter
Piping gun with decorative tips for
   frosting and spreads
Ice cube trays
Vegetable peeler
Basting brushes

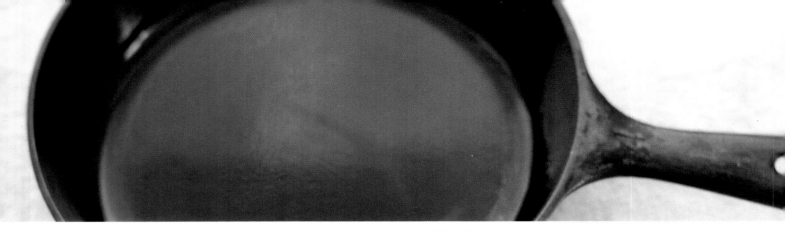

Care for a Cast Iron Skillet

A well-seasoned cast iron skillet is as slippery as any non-stick pan and is a wonderful surface to cook eggs, crepes, quick sautés and cakes. To get the most of your cast iron, follow these tips for proper care.

1. Your cast iron pans should always have a slick, shiny finish. To maintain these qualities, never scrub your pans with abrasive soap or scrubbing sponges or place in the dishwasher. Simply rinse the pan in hot water, use a scrapper if needed and then dry thoroughly with a paper towel.

2. Cast iron cookware loves to be oiled. After every third use, or when needed, simply rub olive oil or coconut oil on your clean, dry cast iron pan using a paper towel. For an intense moisture boost when your cast iron has become rough and dull, rub them generously with olive oil and then place them in a warm (170°) oven for 2-4 hours.

3. Use your cast iron cookware for quick cooking foods such as eggs, crepes, quick cooking meats, stir fried veggies and reheating meals. Avoid preparing slow-cooked foods and acidic foods, such as tomatoes and vinegar, in cast iron. Acidic foods will strip the pan and can lead to rusting. ✍

Nourishing Essentials

Boost your Body with the Regular Consumption of Nourishing Foods

Nourishing foods are health enhancing foods. This chapter provides insight, tidbits and guidelines to help you understand and incorporate nourishing foods into your daily diet. As you browse through this recipe guide you will witness that the delicious dishes I've created are composed of a lovely combination of nourishing foods. The *Ingredient Index* (pg 137) will help to transform these healthy foods into amazing dishes.

4 Nourishing Essentials

1. *Premium produce* (pg 14)
2. *Super nuts, seeds, legumes and grains* (pg 14)
3. *Cultured dairy and fermented foods* (pg 23)
4. *Roasted beef bone and chicken broth* (pg 26)

Nourishing Food #1: Premium Produce, Nature's rainbow to good health

Below is a list of nutrient-packed produce items that are a natural source of nourishment. Each week I fill my shopping cart with 6 or more premium produce items that are on sale and in season, organic and locally grown. These premium produce items become the inspiration for my weekly meals. I have suggested "organic" for the items that are typically the dirtiest when conventionally grown.

Organic arugula
Avocado
Asparagus
Organic beets
Organic berries
Organic peaches
Organic apricots
Organic nectarines
Organic plums
Papaya
Organic hearty greens
(spinach, chard, kale)
Cauliflower
Yam

Organic broccoli
Brussels sprouts
Cabbages (green,
purple, napa,
bok choy)
Organic chili peppers
(sweet bells and hot)
Organic carrots
Organic cherries
Citrus fruits
Jicama
Organic kale
Organic summer
squash

Winter squash/pumpkin
Kiwi
Parsnips
Turnips
Kohlrabi
Mango
Organic apples
Organic pears
Sweet corn
Persimmon
Pineapple
Organic tomatoes

Nourishing Food #2: Super Nuts, Seeds, Legumes and Grains

Each "seed" (nuts, grains, legume) requires a slightly different process for soaking and cooking. Follow the specific guidelines on the following pages for success.

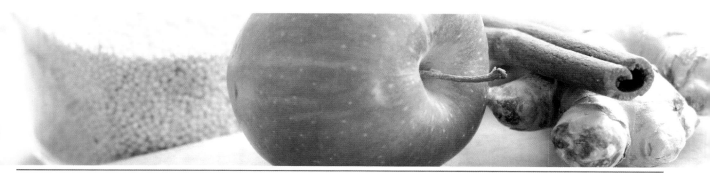

Super-Toasty Nuts and Seeds

These nuts and seeds are called "super-toasty" because, once prepared, they are a delicious crunchy super food, perfect for snacking, baking and topping so many different foods. Many of the recipes throughout this book will ask for them. I like to have two different types of Super-Toasty Nuts and Seeds available in my pantry. Simply stock up on raw nuts and seeds when they are on sale at the market. Soak them in water for 8-12 hours, drain, dehydrate them in the oven overnight, cool and store. My children love to nibble them fresh and warm from the oven!

Ingredients:

Nuts or seeds such as pecans, walnuts, sunflower seeds and almonds

Filtered water
Sea salt (optional)

1. Using a glass container, combine the raw nuts or seeds with filtered water to soak. For every 1 cup of nuts or seeds stir in 2 cups filtered water and ½ tsp. sea salt.
2. Cover the container and allow the nuts or seeds to soak at room temperature for 8-12 hours. Drain and rinse the seeds and nuts. Heat the oven at the lowest temperature possible, preferably no higher than 160°. Spread the nuts and seeds on a lined baking sheet in a single layer and place them in the warm oven. It should take 8-14 hours, depending on the size of nut or seed. Cool and store them in a sealed glass container. ℰ℧

Cook's Note: The seeds and nuts that I have suggested work best when soaked and toasted. They are used in a variety of ways in many of my recipes. Peanuts, pumpkin seeds, cashews and flaxseeds also will NOT soak well.

Toasted Nuts, Seeds and Flaked Coconut

Toasting nuts, seeds and coconut accentuates the natural flavors. I personally prefer the "Super-toasty" (pg 15) way but this is the basic method if you are in a pinch or are cooking with nuts and seeds that do not soak well.

1. Preheat the oven 350°.
2. Spread the nuts, seeds or coconut flakes out on a baking sheet and place in the heated oven for 5-7 minutes until slightly toasted.
3. Allow to cool; store in an air tight glass container. ℘

. . . .

Super Soaked Beans, Peas and Lentils

Beans, Peas, Lentils and even peanuts, fall into the same seed category known as legumes. Legumes are seeds that form in a pod. Most legumes or "beans" can be purchased dried or canned in the store. There are many benefits to soaking and cooking dried legumes yourself rather than purchasing them canned from the store. I find that dried beans such as pinto, kidney and black beans are best to soak, fully cook and then add to your favorite recipe. I like to soak and cook a large batch of beans and then store them in the freezer in standard can-size portions (approximately 1 ¾ cup, which equals one 15 ounce can).

Lentils and peas, on the other hand, can be soaked and then cooked directly in a recipe because they cook rather quickly. Lentils can also be cooked plain, chilled and then added to a salad. Check out the methods on page 17 for preparing legumes at home.

Why Kick The Can?
The benefits of cooking your beans at home.
Less waste
Saves money
Cleaner beans, free of any added preservatives and can residues
They store easily in the freezer.
Soaking beans prior to cooking them helps to release the vital nutrients within

The Dry Bean to Cooked Bean Equation

Because beans vary in size and texture there is a slight variation in the quantity yielded from cooking dried beans. In general, the best ratio for cooking beans is:

Every ⅔ cup dry beans = approximately 1 ¾ cup cooked beans=1-15 ounce can

Soaking and Cooking Dried Beans and other Legumes

Ingredients:
Bean, pea or lentil of choice

Warm filtered water
Time

1. Measure the amount of dried beans (legumes) you plan to prepare. Below you will find a chart that shows the measured amounts of dried beans to water ratio and cooking time. In general, add 2 cups filtered water for every ⅔ cup dried beans. Rinse the dried beans in a colander, remove any foreign debris. Transfer the clean beans to a large pot or glass storage container and add the water. Cover the beans and allow them to soak for the necessary amount of time (refer to the chart). The beans are ready to cook when they have doubled in size and are slightly tender. Change the water every 12 hours, if needed. Typically this will take between 6-24 hours depending on the type of bean.

2. Drain and rinse the soaked beans. Transfer the soaked beans to a pot that they will be cooked in. Season with sea salt and bring the beans to a boil over high heat and then reduce the heat to low, partially cover, and cook until tender. Add herbs, onion, garlic and olive oil to the pot for enhanced flavor and texture. Skim off any foam that accumulates at the top of the cooking beans. Once cooked, drain the beans from their cooking liquid. Use the cooked beans for recipes or store them in the fridge for up to 7 days or in the freezer for up to 5 months. ∞

Dried Bean and Legume Soaking and Cooking Guidelines

Legume Type	Bean to Water Ratio	Soak Time	Cooking Time
Black eye peas	1:4	7-14 hours	1-2 hours
Black bean	1:3	7-14 hours	1-2 hours
Cannellini Beans	1:4	7-14 hours	1-2 hours
Garbanzo beans	1:4	8-24 hours	3-4 hours
Great Northern Beans	1:3	7-14 hours	2-3 hours
Kidney beans	1:4	8-24 hours	1-2 hours
Lentils	1:2	6-12 hours	20-40 min
Lima Beans	1:4	8-24 hours	1-2 hours
Navy Beans	1:4	8-24 hours	2-3 hours
Pinto beans	1:4	8-24 hours	2-3 hours
Red Beans	1:4	8-24 hours	2-3 hours

Vanessa's Kitchen – Pure Food Joy!

Super Soaked Grains

The simple soaking process strips away nutrient inhibitors and awakens the life juice of the grain. Soaking your grains improves taste, texture and digestibility of the grain. See below for proper soaking and cooking methods for each type of grain.

Ingredients:

Grains (millet, quinoa, brown rice, wild rice, buck wheat groats, rolled oats, steel cut oats)

Filtered water

½ Tbsp. whey (see pg 24), plain yogurt or apple cider vinegar (this will help to clean and break down the starches in the grain)

1. Plan to soak grains the morning or evening prior to cooking. Allow for 8-14 hours soak time.
2. Measure the desired amount of whole grain needed to prepare your dish. Rinse the grains using a colander and place it in a bowl or directly in the pot in which they will be cooked. Then stir in the water and whey. See the chart below for proper grain to water ratios.
3. Cover the soaking grains and let rest for 8-14 hours at room temperature. They can be cooked immediately in the soaking pot, simply add sea salt and cook. The soaked grains can also be drained, rinsed and then cooked in a new liquid or placed in a soup, stew or casserole recipe. ℘

Guidelines for Soaking and Cooking Whole Grains

Type	Grain: Liquid	Sea Salt	Soak Time	Cook Time	Final Yield
Buckwheat groats	1 cup: 2 cups	¼ tsp.	8-12 hrs.	20-25 min.	2 ½ cups
Long Grain Brown Rice	1 cup: 2 cups	¼ tsp.	8-16 hrs.	35-40 min.	2 ½ cups
Short Grain Brown Rice	1 cup: 2 ½ cups	¼ tsp.	8-16 hrs.	40-45 min.	3 cups
Wild Rice	1 cup: 2 ½ cups	½ tsp.	8-16 hrs.	45-50 min.	4 cups
Millet	1 cup: 2 ½ cups	½ tsp.	8-12 hrs.	15 min.	3 ½ cups
Quinoa	1 cup: 2 cups	¼ tsp.	8-16 hrs.	15-20 min.	2 ¾ cups
Rolled Oats	1 cup: 3 cups	¼ tsp.	6-12 hrs.	5 min.	2 cups
Steel Cut Oats	1 cup: 3 ½ cups	½ tsp.	8-14 hrs.	25-30 min.	3 cups

Cook's Note:
If the grains have NOT been soaked prior to cooking, then add five more minutes to your cooking time.

Let cooked whole grains rest for 5-10 minutes covered in the pan prior to serving.

Prep Time:
10 minutes

Cook Time:
40 minutes

Yields:
6-8 servings

Cajun Rice

This recipe is an easy way to give your brown rice a flavorful lift, transforming it into the perfect side to so many Caribbean style dishes.

Ingredients:

3 Tbsp. butter or coconut oil
1 medium onion, minced
½ tsp. sea salt
1 tsp. chili powder
¾ tsp. ground cumin
½ tsp. garlic powder

1 cup brown rice, rinsed
2 cups water
½ Tbsp. whey, plain yogurt, or cider vinegar (optional)
Fresh lime juice (optional)

Suggested Pairings:
Grilled Cajun Chicken Drummies (pg 42), Grilled Mahi Mahi (pg 94), Coconut Lime Truffles (pg 112)

1. Warm a medium size pot over medium heat. Add the butter, onion, salt, chili powder, cumin and garlic powder; sauté for 2-3 minutes. Then add the rice and continue to sauté for 1-2 minutes longer. Add the water and whey to the rice, cover with a lid, remove the pan from the heat and allow the rice to set for up to 10 hours before cooking (this is optional but the longer the rice rests, the more flavors it will absorb.)

2. When ready to cook, remove the lid from the rice and bring it to a simmer over medium heat, reduce the heat to low, cover the pot and cook for 35-40 minutes. Let the rice rest for 5-10 minutes then gently fluff with a fork, drizzle with lime juice and serve. ℘

Prep Time:
10 minutes

Soak Time:
8-24 hours

Cook Time:
5 minutes

Yields:
2-4 servings

Overnight Oats

Rolled Oats are very absorbent. They will absorb their soaking liquid and become soft while they rest. Therefore I treat them a little differently than other grains by preparing the soaking liquid with a natural sweetener, spices and add a tablespoon of cultured dairy to help break down the starches. Once oats are soaked for 8-24 hours, I simply warm them before eating. No "cooking" necessary. I like to prepare mine before I go to bed so they can be enjoyed the next morning. This is the basic recipe. The flavors can be adjusted depending on what type of sweetener, spices and extracts are used.

Suggested Pairings:
Scrambled Eggs
(pg 36), Favorite
Family Frittata
(pg 49), Maple Whip
(pg 126), prepared
ham, sausage
or bacon

Ingredients:

¾ cup traditional rolled oats

¾ cup filtered water

¼ tsp. sea salt

1 Tbsp. whey or plain yogurt

½ cup milk or additional water

¼ cup organic whole fruit preserves
(blueberry or strawberry) or pure
maple syrup

1 tsp. pure almond or vanilla extract
(optional)

½ tsp. ground cinnamon (optional)

Super-toasty (pg 15) or toasted
nuts or coconut (pg 16),
roughly chopped (optional)

Dried fruits (optional)

1. Place the oats, water, salt, whey, milk, preserves, extract and spices in a medium size sauce pan or a jar. Stir until well combined. Cover it with a lid and allow the oats to soak for 8-24 hours in the fridge.

2. Enjoy the soaked oats cold or warm them for 5 minutes on the stove. Top them with super-toasty nuts or coconut and enjoy! ℬ

Nourishing food #3: Cultured Dairy and Fermented Foods

Cultured dairy and fermented foods have existed for thousands of years and are a staple in many cultures throughout the world today. They are a natural source of probiotics. I always have organic plain whole milk yogurt and/or sour cream on hand in my fridge to use for homemade dressings, marinades, sauces, snacks, baking, garnishes and sides. Plain whole milk yogurt can even be easily transformed into *Honey Yogurt* (pg 24), *Homemade Greek Yogurt* (pg 24), *Cultured Cream Cheese* (pg 25) and *Whey* (pg 25).

Naturally fermented foods such as "raw" sauerkraut and pickles are also loaded with probiotics. I like to have these on hand as a refreshing, tangy topper or side for a variety of dishes. Raw krauts, pickles and other fermented foods help to maintain a healthy digestive tract. Raw apple cider vinegar is also a naturally fermented food.

Cultured Dairy

The most common cultured dairy products are yogurt, kefir, buttermilk, and sour cream. These products have been preserved through a natural process called lacto-fermentation. The lacto-fermentation process is caused by healthy, active living cultures that have been added to or that naturally form in fresh milk and cream. These "active cultures" are a source of probiotics that break down difficult-to-digest milk proteins such as casein. As a result, cultured dairy products provide an easier way for our bodies to absorb and digest the essential nutrients provided in dairy plus provide a dose of probiotics.

The benefits of marinating raw meats and grains with cultured products

Marinating meats and grains in a bit of cultured dairy or raw apple cider vinegar prior to cooking and consuming them can enhance the digestibility and texture. The active living cultures will begin to break down the heavy starches and proteins before we enjoy them. I like to use either yogurt or sour cream in my baked goods, then let the batter rest at room temperature for 2-3 hours prior to baking. I also will add 2-3 tsp. of whey or yogurt to my meat marinades and soaking grains (see pg 19).

Honey Yogurt

Prep Time:
5 minutes

Yields:
2 ½ cups yogurt

Ingredients:

2 cups plain whole milk yogurt
½ cup raw honey
1 ½ tsp. pure almond or vanilla extract

Fresh or dried fruits and toasted nuts
or coconut for topping

1. In quart sized container, mix together the yogurt, honey and almond extract. Serve with your favorite cakes and sweet breakfast dishes or prepare fruit parfaits for a healthy treat. ℘

Cook's Note:
I sweeten plain yogurt at home with either raw honey or organic whole fruit preserves. By doing this I know my family will enjoy the right amount of quality sugars.

Homemade Greek Yogurt

Prep Time:
15 minutes

Rest Time:
5-6 hours

Yields:
1 ½ cups whey
2 ½ cups yogurt

Ingredients and Tools:

1 quart plain whole milk yogurt
1 medium sized colander that will
rest over a large bowl
1 large bowl
1 cheese cloth or clean dish towel
½ cup raw honey or organic whole
fruit preserves (optional)

1 ½ tsp. pure vanilla or almond extract
(optional)
1-2 Tbsp. unsweetened cocoa powder
(optional)
Dried or fresh fruits, chocolate
pieces, toasted nuts or coconut
(optional)

1. Rest the colander on top of the large bowl so there is a space between the bowl and the colander. Line the colander with the cheesecloth or dish towel. Pour the yogurt into the lined colander and allow it to drain for 5-6 hours at room temperature.

2. Once separated, remove the yogurt from the cloth and place it in a medium mixing bowl. Add the honey or preserves and extract. Using an electric mixer, whip the yogurt on high speed for 1-2 minutes. Then transfer to a container and store it in the fridge. Enjoy this plain or with your favorite fruit and crunchy topping such as Super Snack Mix (pg 65) or Toasted Coconut (see pg 15).

3. The whey can be stored in a glass jar in the fridge for up to 2 weeks. (see pg 25 for uses). ℘

Prep Time:
15 minutes

Rest Time:
9 hours

Yields:
2 cups whey
2 cups cheese

Cultured Cream Cheese

Plain whole milk yogurt can easily be transformed into a cultured cream cheese that makes a lovely, nourishing spread.

Ingredients and Tools:

1 quart plain whole milk yogurt
1 medium sized colander that will
   rest over a large bowl

1 large bowl
1 cheese cloth or clean dish towel
Fresh herbs or raw honey (optional)

1. Rest the colander on top of the large bowl so there is a space between the bowl and the colander. Line the colander with the cheesecloth or dish towel. Pour the yogurt into the lined colander and allow it to drain for 5-6 hours at room temperature.
2. Gather the cheesecloth on the edges and twist it closed around the curds to ring out any excess whey. Let this rest in the colander for another 3-4 hours, ringing the cloth every hour or so to remove more whey.
3. Once separated, store the whey in a jar in the fridge for future use. Keep the cheese plain or mix it with fresh herbs and pipe it onto fresh veggies or mix it with raw honey for a tangy, sweet spread. Wrap the cheese in parchment or wax paper and store it in the fridge for up to 3 weeks. Transfer the whey to a glass jar and store in the fridge for up to 3 months. ✑

. . . .

The Ways of Whey

What is whey? Whey is the almost-clear liquid that can be separated from the white solid substance (curds) found in yogurts and sour cream. Whey has active cultures that can benefit our digestive tract and it can help to break down fibers in raw meats and grains prior to cooking (see soaking grains pg 19). Whey can also be sipped or added to beverages for a probiotic boost. ✑

Naturally Fermented Foods

Raw sauerkraut is the most common source of naturally fermented food found in the market. It is always found in the refrigerated section of the market. Sauerkraut that is found on the shelf at the market has been preserved by heat, which eliminates the natural probiotics.

Raw sauerkraut is prepared from a combination of fresh cabbage and sea salt that is allowed to ferment at room temperature. The natural fermentation process creates an abundance of healthy bacteria that provide a nourishing boost to our bodies. I like to enjoy a few bites on the side with my protein meals for a digestive aid. ℘

Nourishing Food #4: Beef Bone and Chicken Broth

Beef bone broth and chicken broths are an optimum choice for whole body healing. Homemade broth is a natural remedy that can transform into a wide variety of dishes. Broths can be easily stored in the fridge and freezer. Check the following pages for my favorite ways to prepare and enjoy these timeless nourishing treasures. ℘

Roasted Beef Bone Broth

The best way to acquire beef bones for broth is to ask your local butcher for them. The other option is to purchase a portion of a beef from a local farmer that will come with all the cuts of meat plus bones to make a rich broth. Bone broths are nourishing because they are a source of alkaline minerals that can help to prevent inflammation.

Ingredients:

3-4 pounds beef bones

Olive oil

2 large carrots

2-3 stalks of celery

1 large onion

6-8 crushed and peeled garlic cloves

1 bunch of parsley

1-2 bay leaves

2-3 Tbsp. white wine or apple cider vinegar

14-16 cups water

Sea salt and pepper to taste

*Cook's Note:
This recipe will make a very clean broth that is good for sipping. Sometimes the bones have meat still on them. In this case I like to make Veggie Beef Soup, see the recipe on pg 28.*

1. First roast the bones. Preheat the oven 375°. Place the bones on a baking sheet and drizzle them with olive oil. Place them in the heated oven and allow them to roast for 50-60 minutes.

2. Place the roasted beef bones in a large stock pot along with the carrots, celery, onion, garlic, parsley, bay leaves and wine. Cover them with the water and bring the pot to a simmer over high heat. Reduce the heat to low and continue to simmer the stock, partially covered, for 3-4 hours.

3. Cool the finished stock; remove the bones and veggies by pouring the stock through a large colander that is placed over another large stock pot. The broth can be seasoned with salt and pepper, to taste, and it will last in the fridge for up to 10 days or in the freezer for 8 months. Enjoy it as a warm, nourishing beverage, use as a base for soups and stews, or for poaching eggs and veggies for a healthy, hearty meal. (see recipe pg 28)

Veggie Beef Soup

I like to transform this soup into a complete meal by
poaching fresh organic greens such as spinach, chard or kale.

Ingredients:

2-3 pounds beef bones with meat
Olive oil
4 stalks of celery, chopped
1 large onion, diced
1 bell pepper or chili, diced (optional)
6 cloves garlic, minced
¾ cup minced parsley
1-2 bay leaves

2-3 Tbsp. white wine or apple cider
  vinegar
10-12 cups water
3 carrots, sliced
1 ¾ cup cooked beans, diced turnips
  or parsnips
1 28-ounce can diced tomatoes
Sea salt and pepper to taste

*Cook's Note:
To make **Poached
Greens n Eggs in
Broth** simply bring
the veggie beef soup
to a simmer, stir in
chopped chard,
kale or spinach,
and simmer for 1-2
minutes. Then crack
2-4 eggs into the
broth and simmer
until poached
medium. Serve with
toast, a sprinkle
of cheese and chili
flakes.*

1. First roast the bones. Preheat the oven 375°. Place the bones in a large baking dish
   and drizzle them with olive oil and season with salt and pepper. Place them in the
   heated oven and allow them to roast for 50-60 minutes.

2. Place the roasted beef bones in a large stock pot along with the celery, onion,
   pepper, garlic, parsley, bay leaves and wine. Cover them with the water and bring
   the pot to a simmer over high heat. Reduce the heat to low and continue to
   simmer the stock, partially covered, for 2 hours. Add the carrots, beans, or other
   veggies and diced tomatoes; continue to cook for 2-3 hours until the meat is very
   tender.

3. Once cooked, remove the beef bones from the broth and allow to cool. Remove
   the meat from the bones and add it to the soup. Discard the bones and the bay
   leaves. Season with salt and pepper to taste. Store in the fridge for up to 10 days,
   or in the freezer for 8 months. Enjoy it with poached greens and eggs, cooked
   pasta or a whole grain and a sprinkle of sharp Italian cheese.

Classic Roast Chicken with Stock

A classic roast chicken will provide a warm, nourishing meal and a staple base
for a wide variety of dishes such as soups, chilies, salads and casseroles.

Prep Time:
15 minutes

Bake Time:
1 ½-2 hours

Ingredients:

1 3-5 pound organic or free range
chicken

Sea salt and pepper (roughly 2-3 tsp.
sea salt and a ½ tsp. pepper)

Garlic powder

1 large onion, quartered

5-6 large garlic cloves, peeled and
crushed with a large knife

1 handful fresh parsley

2-3 tsp. dry sage or
2-3 Tbsp. fresh sage

1-2 tsp. dry rosemary and/or thyme
or 1 sprig fresh (optional)

2 stalks celery or carrots or 1 of each

1 bay leaf

2 cups water

1-2 Tbsp. butter or olive oil

1. Preheat the oven 400°. Season the chicken inside and out with salt, pepper and
   garlic powder.
2. Fill the cavity of the chicken with ½ of the quartered onion, 4 cloves of garlic,
   parsley, sage, rosemary and thyme.
3. Assemble a vegetable roasting rack in the bottom of a roasting pan with the
   carrots and celery. Place the chicken breast side down on the veggie rack. Add
   the remaining onion and garlic to the pan along with the bay leaf and water.
   Cover and place in the lower portion of the heated oven. Reduce the oven
   temperature to 350° and cook for 1 hour. Then uncover the chicken and bake for
   an additional 30-40 minutes or until the internal temperature has reached 170°.
   For a crispy, golden skin and traditional presentation, turn the chicken breast side
   up, dab the top with butter and roast, uncovered, for the last 30-40 minutes of
   baking. Allow the chicken to rest for 10-15 minutes, covered, before serving.
4. Enjoy the roasted chicken for a meal with gravy (made with the pan juices) and
   mashed potatoes, or, allow it to cool and remove the majority of the meat
   from the carcass to use for other meals during the week. Use the remaining
   carcass and roasting stock to prepare *Chicken Broth* (pg 30) for soups and
   casseroles.

*Cook's Note:
The pan juices from
the roasted chicken
are a stock that is
rich and tasty and
becomes the perfect
base for a soothing
broth or a rich
gravy. There are so
many delicious and
nourishing meals
that can evolve from
a roasted chicken.*

Prep Time:
25 minutes

Cook Time:
3 hours,
stove top;
6 hours,
slow cooker

Yields:
10-12 cups broth

Chicken Broth

Ingredients:

1 roasted chicken carcass with the
  roasting stock (see pg 29)

12-14 cups filtered water for the stock
  pot, 8-10 cups for the slow cooker

½ cup dry white wine (optional)

1 large onion, quartered

2-3 large carrots and/or parsnips

2-3 celery stalks

8 cloves of garlic, peeled and crushed

1 handful of fresh parsley

1-2 sprigs fresh rosemary, thyme and/
  or sage (optional)

1-2 bay leaf

1 tsp. peppercorns or ground black
  pepper

1 Tbsp. sea salt

*Cook's Note:
I like to prepare a
Turkey Broth
using the same
recipe and my
leftover turkey
carcass. I often
freeze the carcass
after the holiday
until I am ready to
prepare the broth.*

1. Place all of the ingredients in a large stock pot. Bring to a boil, reduce to medium-low, partially cover, and simmer for 3 hours. For the slow cooker, add all the ingredients and set the slow cooker on high for 6 hours.

2. Cool the broth. Using colander that fits over another large pot or bowl, separate the broth from the other ingredients. If preparing a chicken soup, reserve pieces of the cooked chicken and slice the cooked carrots to add back into the soup. (see recipe pg 31)

3. Store the broth in the fridge for up to 6 days and in the freezer for up to 6 months. Use the broth to prepare soups and entrees of your choice. Store the broth in 2-4 cup portions so it is ready for future recipes. 🙬

Prep Time:
50 minutes

Cook Time:
4 hours

Yields:
10-12 servings

Chicken Vegetable Soup

When the cold season sets in, this warm soother will provide warm healing from within.

Ingredients:

1 recipe Chicken Broth
(see pg 30)

1 ¾ cup (1 15-ounce can) cooked great
northern beans, cooked brown
rice or cooked pasta

2 cups cooked carrots (can use
the carrots that were used in
the Roasted Chicken Broth
preparation)

2 cups cooked shredded chicken

1 cup fresh peas or 3-4 cups fresh
baby spinach leaves

½ cup minced parsley

1-2 lemons, juiced

Salt and pepper to taste

Grated sharp italian cheese
(optional garnish)

1. Prepare the Roasted Chicken Stock (see pg 29). It is best to roast your chicken
the day before making the stock.

2. Heat the prepared stock and add the beans, carrots, chicken, peas or spinach and
parsley to the pot. Simmer for 10-15 minutes, then stir in the lemon juice and salt
and pepper to taste.🍜

Vanessa's Kitchen - Pure Food Joy!

Simple Proteins

Essential protein accompaniments for fast and easy meals.

    This chapter showcases easy-to-prepare proteins. A variety of meats and different methods for eggs that cook quickly and pair perfectly with many seasonal veggie, fruit and whole grain dishes that are on hand in the fridge. The proteins that I have suggested will cook up fast with a skillet, pan, broiler or grill.

    I recommend shopping the sales and keeping a stock of these protein items in your fridge and freezer so they are ready to grab, prepare and pair with the suggested breakfast dish, Sensational Side or Salad to make each meal fast, healthy and delicious!

Simple Proteins to stock-up on

Farm fresh or organic eggs

Naturally cured bacon

Natural or organic chicken
  tenderloins

Natural or organic chicken breasts

Natural or organic chicken legs

Wild caught Pacific Salmon Filet

White fish fillet such as tilapia,
  northern Pacific Cod or halibut

Raw peeled shrimp

Pork Tenderloin Cutlets

All-natural pork chops

Grass fed or organic beef steaks

Lamb chops

Prep Time:
20 minutes

Cook Time:
4-5 hours

Hard Boiled Eggs

What is the best way to hard boil an egg? Here is my suggestion; I hope it works for you!
A little tip, older eggs will peel easier than new eggs.

Method:

1. Place the eggs in a sauce pan. Be sure the eggs are snug; too much rolling in the pan will cause cracking during cooking. Choose your pan size accordingly. Add water to the pan until the eggs are covered.
2. Bring water and eggs to a boil over medium-high heat on the stove. Once the eggs begin to boil, turn off the heat and let the eggs rest in the hot water for 10-15 minutes. Then drain the eggs and rinse them in cool water.
3. Allow the eggs to come to room temperature before peeling or chilling for future use. ℘

Egg O's and Avo's

A fun, simple and nourishing breakfast for young and old.

Ingredients:

1-2 hard-boiled eggs, peeled   **Sea salt**
1 ripe avocado, cut into slices

1. Slice the hard boiled eggs into circles to look like eyes and a nose.
2. Arrange the pieces of the sliced egg on the plate to make a face. Use the avocado slices to make the mouth. Sprinkle with sea salt and serve. ℘

Cook's Note:
Have fun adding
more colorful
veggies to
this simply
healthy dish.

Soft Boiled Eggs

If you enjoy a juicy yolk and want to avoid the frying pan,
soft boiled eggs are the perfect choice.

1. Place the amount of eggs that you would like to enjoy in a small sauce pan. Remember to fit them snuggly to avoid cracking. Cover them eggs completely with water and bring them to a boil, over medium-high heat. Once the water begins to boil, set a timer for 2 minutes.
2. When 2 minutes is up, immediately drain the eggs and rinse them quickly in cool water. Crack the eggs in half using a teaspoon. Enjoy the egg right out of the shell with a dash of sea salt and pepper and hot sauce, too.

Prep Time:
5 minutes

Suggested Pairings:
Baked Bacon
(pg 37),
Homemade
Chorizo (pg 44),
fresh tomato and
Honey Yogurt
(pg 24)

Fried Eggs

One, two, or a few? A hot, fried egg with a runny yolk tastes great on top of so many
quick veggie sautés or simply served with a piece of toast and a salad. A nutrient-rich
protein that cooks up so fast!

Method:

Heat a heavy bottomed skillet over medium-high heat. Use ghee or a combination of butter and olive oil to coat the pan. Add the eggs to the hot pan, reduce the heat to low, cover the eggs with a lid and allow them to cook until the white is set and the yolk is how you like it.

Scrambled Eggs

Each day, this is the base of our quick breakfast before we run out the door. Our son
cooks them up for the family in no time.

Ingredients:

2-6 eggs

1-2 Tbsp. milk

Sea salt and pepper to taste

Olive oil and butter or ghee (to coat the pan)

Shredded cheese (optional)

Prep Time:
3 minutes

Cook Time:
3-5 minutes

1. Crack your eggs into a bowl add the milk, salt and pepper and lightly whisk them together.
2. Heat a seasoned iron skillet over medium heat. Add a combination of butter and olive oil or ghee to the pan. When pan is coated and hot, add the eggs. After 1 minute of cooking, turn the eggs using a spatula. The add the cheese to the eggs and continue to cook until the eggs are set.

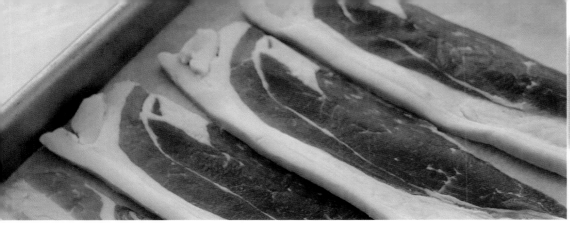

Baked Bacon

I do believe this is the easiest and most efficient way to cook bacon. Give it a try, you'll love it!

Ingredients:

½-1 pound naturally cured bacon

1. Preheat the oven to 375°. Line a large baking sheet with parchment paper for easy clean up. Cut the bacon into the size you prefer and place it on the prepared baking sheet.
2. Place the pan in the hot oven and bake for 7-10 minutes. Then turn the oven off and let the bacon rest in the hot oven for 3-5 minutes longer, or until cooked to your desired crispness.
3. Remove the pan from the oven, transfer the cooked bacon to a shallow dish lined with paper towels to absorb the excess grease. If you like, drain the remaining bacon grease from the sheet pan into a jar and store in the fridge for up to two weeks for additional cooking uses.

Cook's Note:
For efficiency and less mess, I prepare **breakfast sausage** *this way too. I place my patties or links in a baking dish with ½ inch of water and bake in a heated 375° oven for 20-30 minutes or until browned and cooked through.*

Seasoning for Meat and Fish

There are 3 ingredients for a basic seasoning that will make meats and fish taste great whether cooked up quick on the grill, in a skillet or in the broiler.

Sea salt
Garlic powder
Ground pepper

Lightly sprinkle the meat and use olive oil, butter, ghee or coconut oil to cook them up fast. &

- -

Broiled White Fish

A lovely, light protein that is easy to prepare.

Ingredients:

Tilapia, North Pacific cod fish filet, or halibut	**Olive oil**
Sea salt	**Butter**
Ground black pepper	**Grated parmesan cheese (optional)**
Garlic powder	**Fresh lemon (optional)**
	Arugula (optional)

1. If your broiler is in the main part of your oven, then position rack on the upper ⅓ portion of your oven. Heat the broiler to high heat.
2. Have ready a baking sheet lined with parchment paper or a piece of aluminum foil drizzled with olive oil. Rinse the raw fish, dry gently with a paper towel and place it on the baking sheet. Season the fish with salt, pepper and garlic powder. Then place 1-2 tsp. butter on top of each fish filet.
3. Place the fish under the broiler for 7-12 minutes or until cooked through, golden and crispy on the edges. Serve with fresh lemon and arugula. &

Prep Time:
5 minutes

BroilTime:
7-12 minutes

*Cook's Note:
Broiled White Fish pairs well with Pico Di Gallo (pg 52), Everyday Italian Salad (pg 88), and Eggplant Puttenesca (pg 103). You can also make it a **Parmesean Crusted White Fish** by topping the fish with grated parmesan cheese for the last 2 minutes of cooking.*

Skillet Shrimp

Buttery bites that taste so good popped out of the pan and into your mouth.

Ingredients:

1 pound raw medium sized shrimp,
    peeled and deveined
3 Tbsp. butter
1-2 cloves garlic minced
Sea salt and pepper
½ cup minced fresh parsley
⅓ cup minced chives (optional)
Chili flakes or hot sauce (optional)

Shredded parmesan cheese
    (optional)
1 cup diced fresh tomatoes
    (optional)
1-2 cups baby spinach or arugula
    (optional)
Fresh lemon juice (optional)

Suggested Pairings:
Fresh Fruit with
Marscapone Dip
(pg 61), Warm
Cheese and Artichoke
Dip (pg 64),
Strawberry Lemon
Almond Cream
Cake (pg 116).

1. Have the shrimp cleaned, chilled, and ready to cook. Heat a large skillet over medium heat. Melt the butter and then add the garlic. Let the garlic cook in the butter for 1 minute, then increase the heat to high and add the shrimp to the skillet.

2. Season the shrimp with salt and pepper and sauté continuously for 4-5 minutes or until cooked through. Toss the hot shrimp with fresh herbs, chili flakes, cheese, fresh tomato, lemon and or greens if you like.

Wild Balsamic Salmon

Wild salmon is a great source of healthy fats.

Ingredients:

Wild caught pacific salmon filet
Sea salt
Ground black pepper
Garlic powder

Premium olive oil
Butter
Premium balsamic vinegar
    (see pg 7)

1. If your broiler is in the main part of your oven, then position rack on the upper ⅓ portion of your oven. Heat the broiler to high heat or a grill to med-high heat.
2. Have ready a piece of aluminum foil with the edges folded up. Drizzle with olive oil.
3. Rinse the fish, dry gently with a paper towel and place it on the foil skin side down. Brush the top with balsamic vinegar and season with salt, pepper and garlic powder. Place 1-2 tsp. butter on top of each fish filet. Broil or grill the fish for 7-12 minutes until cooked through.

Cook's Note:
For a delicious and complete meal I like to serve this prepared Balsamic Salmon with Berries, Goat Cheese, chopped pecans, fresh basil and Greens. Drizzle the prepared salad with additional balsamic vinegar, salt and pepper to taste.

Chicken Tenders

This chicken is easy to prepare in a fry pan or on a grill. I like to keep a stock of chicken tenders in my freezer. They thaw and cook up quickly; lean, tasty bites from the skillet.

Ingredients:

All natural or organic chicken tenders or chicken breast (cut into strips)
Sea salt
Ground black pepper
Garlic powder

Butter and olive oil or ghee
Fresh Greens (optional)
Fresh lemon juice or balsamic vinegar (optional)

Suggested Pairings:
Black Bean and Avocado Salad (pg 79), Lemon Veggie Quinoa Salad (pg 82), Coconut Rice Salad with Cilantro Lime Vinaigrette (pg 80), Coconut Lime Truffles (pg 112), Zucchini Fudge Brownies (pg 122)

1. Have the chicken clean and ready to cook. If you have marinated it ahead of time in a cultured dairy product (see pg 23), then wipe the marinade away. Season the chicken on each side lightly with salt, pepper and garlic powder.

2. Preheat the grill or frying pan over medium-high heat. Add butter, olive oil or ghee to the frying pan. Cook the seasoned chicken for 4-5 minutes on each side or until cooked through. For a flavor boost, add lemon juice or balsamic vinegar to the pan and baste for the last minute or two of cooking. Fully cooked chicken should be 180 degrees and firm to the touch. Store the cooked chicken in the fridge to add to salads or enjoy during the week.

Grilled Cajun Chicken Drummies

Soak up the sun and enjoy an easy grilled chicken dinner.

Ingredients:

3 lbs. chicken legs

2 tsp. sea salt

1 ½ tsp. ground cumin

1 ½ tsp. sweet or smoked paprika

1 tsp. garlic powder

½ tsp ground black or ground red cayenne pepper

1. In a large bowl combine together the salt, cumin, garlic powder, paprika and pepper. Add the chicken legs to the bowl and toss until well coated with the spice mixture.
2. Preheat the grill to medium heat (400°). Place the coated chicken drumsticks on the heated grill and cook for 15-20 minutes on each side until cooked though. Serve with your favorite summer side dishes.

Suggested Pairings:
Fresh fruit,
Cajun Rice (pg 21),
Black Bean Corn
and Avocado Salad
(pg 79), Coconut
Rice Salad with
Cilantro Lime
Vinaigrette (pg 80),
Pineapple Blueberry
Slaw (pg 94),
Coconut Lime
Truffles (pg 112).

Prep Time:
10 minutes

Grill Time:
15-20 minutes

Yields:
6-8 servings

Steak and Lamb Chops

A hot broiler or grill is the easiest way to prepare these tasty meats.

Ingredients:

Ribeye, T-bone, porterhouse, strip
   steak or lamb chops
Sea salt

Ground black pepper
Garlic powder
Melted butter

1. Allow the chops or steaks to rest at room temperature for 20 minutes. If the meat was marinated (see pg 23), wipe it away using a paper towel. Season the meat on each side lightly with salt, pepper and garlic powder.

2. For the broiler, position the oven rack in the upper ⅓ portion of the oven and preheat on high. Rub the broiling pan with olive oil, place the steak or chops on the pan and place under the hot broiler. Cook for 7-8 minutes on each side for a medium rare finish. When you flip the meat, brush the top of the steak or chops with melted butter for extra flavor. Remove the meat from the oven, cover it with foil and let it rest for 5-10 minutes before cutting. This will help the juices absorb.

3. If using the grill, preheat the grill to high heat. Place the seasoned steaks or chops on the hot grill and then reduce the temperature to medium. Cover and grill the meat for 4-6 minutes, then flip, brush with butter and continue grilling for an additional 4-6 minutes on each side until it has reached your desired temperature. Let the meat rest on a platter, covered, for 5-10 minutes before cutting. ✆

Suggested Pairings:
Lemon Veggie Quinoa Salad (pg 82), Kale Chopped Salad (pg 84), Everyday Italian Salad (pg 88), Roasted Rosemary Potatoes (pg 96), Maple Balsamic Root Salad (pg 107), Apricot Ricotta Cheesecake with Fresh Fruit (pg 120), Chocolate Raspberry Torte (pg 118).

Homemade Chorizo

Chorizo is so easy to make and so worthwhile since most
store bought chorizo is loaded with unhealthy additives.

Ingredients:

1 lb. ground turkey or pork	1 Tbsp. chili powder
2 Tbsp. adobo sauce (or substitute favorite hot sauce plus ½ tsp. additional smoked paprika)	2 tsp. garlic powder
	1 tsp. ground cumin
	1 tsp. ground cayenne pepper
1 Tbsp. apple cider vinegar	1 tsp. sweet paprika
1 Tbsp. whey or plain whole milk yogurt (optional)	1 tsp. smoked paprika
	1 tsp. dried oregano
1 tsp. sea salt	½ tsp. ground black pepper

Cook's Note:
I like to store
cooked chorizo in
1 cup portions in
my freezer. This way
it is ready for a quick
grab to pair with
prepared eggs,
tacos or nachos.

1. Using a stand mixer with a paddle attachment or a large bowl combine the ground meat along with the adobo sauce, vinegar, whey, salt, chili powder, cumin, cayenne, sweet and smoked paprika, oregano and black pepper. Mix on low speed for 1-2 minutes or use clean dry hand to work the spices into the meat. Once well combined store the meat in the fridge for 8-24 hours before cooking.

2. When ready to cook heat a large skillet with olive oil over medium heat and brown the chorizo until it is cooked through and crumbled. Drain any excess fat and serve.

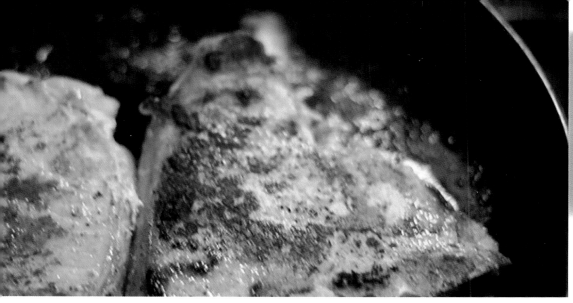

Pan Fried Pork with Apple Glaze

Mmm..mmm...ain't nothing like a hot, juicy pork right out of the pan. An easy apple glaze prepared during the last minutes of cooking makes for a perfect bite.

Ingredients:

Bone in or boneless pork chops or
   sliced pork tenderloin

Sea salt

Ground black pepper

Garlic powder

4-5 Tbsp. apple juice or apple cider

1. Season the pork on each side lightly with salt, pepper and garlic powder.
2. Preheat a large heavy bottomed skillet over medium-high heat. Place the seasoned pork in the pan; reduce the heat to medium and allow them to cook for 3-6 minutes until the bottoms are seared. Flip the pork and sear for 1 minute longer and add the apple juice to the pan. Reduce the heat to medium low, cover and cook the pork for another minute or two until they are cooked through. They should be firm to touch. Serve hot. ℘

Cook's Note:
I like to pair these
tasty chops with
Roasted Winter
Squash (pg 99),
cooked peas and
a seasonal Fruit
Crisp (pg 123). I
always have all my
sides prepared
before cooking the
chops. That way they
can be enjoyed hot
out of the pan.

Breakfast with a Bang!

"Breakfast is the most important meal of the day." There is so much truth to this saying. I've been caught skipping it or going light because I am just not that hungry and then find myself running out of energy by late morning. Taking the time to enjoy a solid breakfast leaves me with a day full of healthy, steady energy. I recommend a balance of proteins, carbs, veggies and or fruits. Feel free to load up because it will burn off during the day. Proteins can take a while to digest; starting the day with them is a wise choice. &

Prep Time:
5 minutes

Cooke Time:
5 minutes

Cheesy Dill Scramblers with Grapefruit and Honey

Scrambled eggs can be done so many wonderful ways. Adding fresh dill and cheese is one of my favorites!

Ingredients:

2-6 farm fresh eggs

1 Tbsp. milk (optional)

Dash of sea salt

Dash of ground black pepper (optional)

1 Tbsp. ghee or 1 Tbsp. butter and 1 Tbsp. extra virgin olive oil

½-1 cup shredded jack, Havarti or muenster or swiss cheese

2-3 sprigs fresh dill, roughly chopped (optional)

2-3 fresh grapefruits

3-4 Tbsp. raw honey

Suggested Pairings:
Baked Bacon (pg 37), Crispy Tater Chips and Onions (pg 101), Baked Banana N Date Bread (pg 113), Carrot Cakes (pg 114)

1. Using a large serrated knife, slice the ends off of the grapefruit, then carefully slice away the outer rind. Cut the grapefruit into circles, starting from one end, then cut the circles in half. Drizzle the slices with raw honey and store in the fridge until ready to serve.

2. Crack the eggs into a medium bowl. Whisk them together with the milk, sea salt and pepper.

3. Heat a large, well-seasoned, cast iron skillet over medium heat. Add the ghee or butter to the warm pan, melt and coat the bottom of the pan. Pour the eggs into the pan and cook for 1-2 minutes. Once slightly set, using a spatula, begin to turn the eggs; add the fresh dill for the last 1-2 minutes of cooking. Serve hot with prepared grapefruit and other sides. ℘

Prep Time:
15 minutes

Cook Time:
15-20 minutes

Yields:
4-6 servings

Family Frittata

A frittata has all the same qualities of a delicious omelet without the fuss of a flip and it can feed more than just a few. This version is my family's favorite.

Ingredients:

6 large eggs
3 Tbsp. milk
2 Tbsp. fresh basil or dill, chopped
½ tsp. sea salt
¼ tsp. pepper
1 Tbsp. butter and 2 Tbsp. olive oil or
    2 Tbsp. ghee
¼ cup minced onion
1 cup chopped asparagus, zucchini
    or chard

1 Tbsp. lemon juice (optional)
½ cup diced ham or cooked chopped
    bacon (optional)
1-2 ounces cream cheese or goat
    cheese, cut into small pieces
½ cup shredded sharp Italian or
    cheddar cheese
Fresh sliced tomato for garnish

Cook's Note: This recipe can be turned into a Breakfast Casserole. Simply double the recipe. Grease and flour a 13 x 9 inch baking dish, place in the cooked veggies, egg mixture and cheeses. Top with shredded cheese and bake for 25-30 minutes in a 350° oven. until set.

1. In a medium bowl, whisk together the eggs, dill, salt and pepper.
2. Heat a 10 inch seasoned cast iron skillet, or oven safe 10 inch skillet, over med-high heat. Add the butter and oil combination, onion and asparagus to the skillet. Season with salt and pepper; sauté for 5 minutes until tender. Reduce the heat to low and add lemon juice and prepared meat; toss to coat. Spread the veggie mixture evenly over the bottom of the pan and pour the egg mixture over the top. Continue to cook on low heat for 5-7 minutes or until the bottom is set and just puffing at the top.
3. Preheat the broiler. Top the frittata with the cream cheese and the shredded Italian cheese. Place the pan under the broiler for 2-3 minutes until the top is set and golden. Serve the frittata cut into wedges, and top with fresh tomato slices.

Berry and Cheese Crepes with Maple-Spiced Nuts

A lovely breakfast treat. Prepare them for your visiting house guests or keep a pan in the fridge for the week's breakfast for the family.

Ingredients:
Have ready at room temperature

Sweet Crepes:
6 large eggs
1 cup milk
⅔ cup whole grain spelt, corn flour, buckwheat flour, all-purpose flour or tapioca flour
¼ cup turbinado sugar, pure cane sugar or coconut sugar
2 Tbsp. whey or plain yogurt (optional)
¾ tsp. sea salt
½ tsp. baking powder
4 Tbsp. melted butter, cooled
Additional butter for the pan

Berry and Cheese Filling:
8 ounces cream cheese or fresh goat cheese (softened)
2 Tbsp. pure cane sugar or pure maple syrup
1 tsp. lemon zest (optional)
1-2 Tbsp. minced mint leaves (optional)
1 cup organic berries

Maple-Spiced Walnuts:
1 cup super-toasty (pg 15) or toasted (pg 16) walnuts or pecans, chopped
½ cup pure maple syrup
1 ½ tsp. ground cinnamon

Suggested Pairings:
Maple Whip (pg 126), Honey Yogurt (pg 24), baked bacon or sausage (pg 37)

1. First prepare the crepe batter. Using a blender or food processor, combine the eggs, milk, flour, whey, sugar, salt, baking powder and melted butter puree until smooth. Let rest at room temperature for up to 8 hours or chill in the fridge for up to 3 days and stir with a whisk before cooking.
2. When ready to cook, have ready a large plate and ten squares of parchment paper to separate the crepes and keep them from sticking together. Heat an 8-10" cast iron skillet (see pg 12 Care for Cast Iron) over med heat. Whisk or blend the crepe batter once again, add a half tablespoon of butter to the hot pan, reduce the temperature to med-low. Coat the bottom of the pan with the butter and then add approximately 1/4 cup of the crepe batter to the pan. Swirl the batter around the pan until the bottom is completely coated. Cook the crepe 1-2 minutes, then flip it and cook for another minute, until set. Transfer the crepe to the large plate. Continue to cook the remaining crepes using the same method, separating each crepe with a small square of parchment paper.
3. Meanwhile, prepare the crepe filling. In a small bowl, combine the cheese, maple syrup, lemon zest and mint. Gently fold in the fresh berries.
5. To assemble the filled crepes, place 3 Tbsp. of the berry and cheese mixture in the center of the crepe and gently roll or fold. Store the filled crepes in the fridge until ready to warm and serve. Place the filled crepes in a warm 350° oven for 15-20 minutes before serving.
6. Meanwhile, in a medium sauce pan combine the walnuts, maple syrup and cinnamon; warm over medium heat. Serve the crepes with the warmed syrup and walnuts and topped with *Honey Yogurt* (pg 24) or fresh whipped cream.

Yields:
6-8 servings,
about
12 crepes

Cook's Note:
*The crepes can be prepared ahead of time and stored in the fridge for everyday wraps and snacks. My kids love **Nut Butter and Jam Crepes**. Simply prepare the sweet crepes above and spread your favorite nut butter and jam in the center and wrap them for a quick, protein rich, breakfast, snack, or lunch.*

Chili N Grits Breakfast Bake with Pico Di Gallo

Your guests will kick up their heels to this dish with a Huevos Rancheros appeal.
Serve it with side of guacamole or sliced avocado. No matter how you slice it,
you're sure to hear a yippee, and a whoo-hoo!

Suggested Pairings:
Guacamole,
Honey Yogurt with
Fruit (pg 24),
Fried Eggs (pg 36),
Carrot Cakes
(pg 114), Zucchini
Fudge Brownies
(pg 122),
Fresh Fruit with
Mascarpone Dip
(pg 61)

Ingredients:

1 Tbsp. butter, ghee or bacon grease
½ cup onion, minced
½ tsp. salt
¼ tsp. pepper
½ tsp. ground cumin (optional)
1 ½ cup water
⅔ cup course ground corn meal
    (aka grits or polenta)
1 cup plain whole milk yogurt or
    sour cream
4 large eggs
3 cups grated extra sharp cheddar
    cheese, divided
½ cup diced roasted green chilies
1 ½ cups cooked, chopped bacon,
    ham, sausage, or
    Homemade Chorizo **(pg 44)**
Minced green onions or chives
    for garnish

Pico Di Gallo:

1 ¼ cup diced fresh tomatoes, seeds
    removed
¾ cup diced avocado or additional
    tomato
1 jalapeno, minced or
    ½ cup minced green pepper
½ cup onion, minced
1 clove garlic minced
2 limes, juiced (4 Tbsp.)
3 Tbsp. apple cider vinegar
1 Tbsp. prepared hot sauce (optional)
¾ tsp. sea salt
¾ cup chopped fresh cilantro

1. Preheat the oven 350°. Grease a 2 qt. 13x9 inch casserole dish with butter.
2. Whisk together the eggs and yogurt and set aside.
3. In a large sauce pan combine the butter, onion, salt, pepper and cumin. Sauté over medium heat until the onion is tender. Then add the water to the pan, bring it to a simmer and gradually whisk in the cornmeal. Whisk continuously for 7-10 minutes until thick and bubbly. Remove from heat and whisk in the egg mixture along with the prepared meat, 1 ½ cup of the cheese and the diced chilies.
4. Pour the mixture into the prepared pan, place in the heated oven and bake for 20 minutes. Remove the pan from the oven and top the grits with the remaining cheese and green onions or chives and bake for an additional 15 minutes.
5. Meanwhile, prepare the Pico Di Gallo by combining together the tomatoes, avocado, chilies, onion, garlic, lime juice, vinegar, hot sauce, salt and cilantro in a medium bowl. Serve with the hot breakfast bake. ᔓ

Yields:
4-6 servings

Cook's Note:
This dish will freeze well. I simply prepare the base layer of Cheesy Grits, cool and freeze. When ready to cook, top the frozen casserole with minced green onion or chives and 1 ½ cup shredded cheddar cheese; bake in a 350° oven for 30 minutes.

Prep Time:
20 minutes

Yields:
6-8 servings

BEST Salad

Breakfast, lunch or dinner, this salad is always a winner! I placed this recipe in the breakfast chapter because it is always a hit at my monthly ladies brunch. My children also love it. The tangy, sweet bacon dressing makes the spinach, egg and other veggies quickly disappear.

Ingredients:

8 ounces uncooked natural bacon

1 small onion, sliced

½ tsp. sea salt

¼ tsp. pepper

½ cup apple cider vinegar

3-4 Tbsp. raw honey

2 Tbsp. plain whole milk yogurt or sour cream

10 ounces baby spinach or spinach mix

4 hard-boiled eggs, peeled and sliced

2 medium tomatoes, sliced into wedges

1 ripe avocado (optional)

¼ cup blue cheese crumbles (optional)

1. Cut the bacon into 1 inch pieces, then cook the bacon in a large skillet until crisp and brown. Reserve the bacon grease.

2. Place ¼ cup of the reserved bacon grease in the pan. Add the onion, salt and pepper; cook over medium heat for 3-5 minutes or until golden and tender. Turn off the heat and add the vinegar, honey and yogurt to the pan.

3. Meanwhile, place the spinach and cooked bacon in a large salad bowl. Pour ½ of the warm onion dressing over and toss, then add the remaining dressing, eggs, and tomatoes and gently toss to coat. Serve immediately ℘

Cook's Note: The dressing for this salad can be prepared the day before serving. Simply follow steps 1-2 then reheat the dressing before tossing the salad.

Snacks & Appetizers

This chapter is full of satisfying snacks and apps that will be enjoyed by all ages. Look for the yummy veggie and fruit dips, super snack mix and other protein bites that will make your heart flip!

These creations can be enjoyed in a variety of ways. They are elegant appetizers, healthy meals for kids, quick snacks and a combination of a few makes a great packed lunch or tapas night. &

Yields:
One 12-ounce
smoothie or
Two 6-ounce
smoothies

Suggested Pairings:
Kale Chips (pg 59),
Popped Corn
(pg 58), Super
Nachos and
Tacos (pg 66)

Fruit Smoothies

Smoothies are a versatile and refreshing, fun snack. They are a super, cool way to
enjoy veggies and fruits, plus nutty proteins and other nourishing supplements.
I always keep a stash of ripe frozen fruit for all my smoothie needs. I stock up on
mangos, berries and bananas when they are a good price in the market. This is a
basic formula for making a successful smoothie. There are so many ways to
create them. Give it a whirl and soon you will discover your family's favorite flavors.
Once you make a few you will be able to eyeball the proportions
and create them in a flash.

Ingredients:

Fruit Base:
3 ounces, about ½ cup, frozen fruit (1 very ripe banana, mango, papaya, pineapple, peaches, apricot, nectarine, melon, or a combination)

Berry Booster:
2 ounces (⅓ cup) frozen organic strawberries, blueberries, raspberries, cherries or blackberries

Protein Booster:
1-2 Tbsp. almond butter, peanut butter, sunflower seed butter or chia seeds

Green Booster: (optional)
½ tsp. spirulina powder or green veggie powder

Veggie Booster: (optional)
2-3 Tbsp. fresh or frozen chopped spinach, shredded raw beet, shredded carrot, or roasted yam

Juice Sweetener:
3-4 ounces (½ cup) naturally sweetened fruit juice. I prefer apple, pear, berry or orange carrot

Additional Sweetener: (optional)
1-2 Tbsp. whole fruit preserves or agave nectar

Smoother:
2-3 ounces (⅓ cup) milk of choice

Probiotic Boost: (optional)
2 Tbsp. kefir or plain whole milk yogurt

Chocolate Boost (optional)
1-2 tsp. unsweetened cocoa powder

Preparation:

Puree all the ingredients together using a hand held blender and a quart size container or a standard blender. Pour into a glass and serve with a straw. For fun, garnish with fresh fruit and whipped cream. ॐ

Popped Corn

My family loves this healthy and economical alternative to typical bagged and boxed snacks found in the store. I usually pick up my organic popping corn from the farmers market or health food store. There are several heirloom varieties, such as black and red, that pop with a lovely crunch.

Suggested Pairings:
Fruit Smoothie
(pg 56), Kale Chips
(pg 59) and Super
Snack Mix (pg 65).

Ingredients:

1 Tbsp. coconut oil

1 Tbsp. olive oil

1/3 cup organic popping corn

3/4 tsp. sea salt

2-3 Tbsp. butter or coconut oil, melted (optional)

1. Have all ingredients ready, pot holders and a large bowl. Place a medium sized, heavy bottomed pot on the stove over medium to high heat. Add the oils and corn to the pan and cover with the lid. Once you hear the kernels begin to pop, begin to shake the pan over the heat and lift it on and off the burner to prevent burning while the corn pops.

2. Once the popping slows, remove the pan from the heat, remove the lid and transfer the hot corn to the large bowl and season with the sea salt. For a tasty flavor drizzle melted butter or coconut oil over the popped corn.

Prep Time:
10 minutes

Roast time:
15-20 minutes

Yields:
2-3 cups
kale chips

Kale Chips

A healthy, light, crispy, salty snack or appetizer.

Ingredients:

**1 bunch kale, cleaned, dried and
chopped (10 cups)**

**2-3 Tbsp. olive oil
1 tsp. course ground sea salt**

1. Preheat the oven 300°.
2. In a large bowl, toss together the kale, olive oil and sea salt.
3. Spread the kale on a large baking sheet and roast for 15 minutes. Then turn the kale and roast 5-10 minutes longer until just crisp and not burned. Serve immediately.

*Cook's Note:
These veggie chips
are light and
delicious! I love
watching my kids
gobble them up
for a snack.
I prefer to pair
them with dried
cranberries for
a sweet contrast.
They taste best
fresh out of the
oven and do not
store well overnight.*

Curry Chicken Salad

Roast the chicken on Sunday and then prepare this tasty salad for the week.
My little ones love this, veggies and all! It is also an elegant addition to a luncheon.

Ingredients:

4 cups roast chicken, shredded (see pg 29)
½ cup shredded carrots
⅓ cup (1 stalk) celery, chopped
½ cup organic raisins or dried currants
2 Tbsp. onion, chopped
3 Tbsp. minced fresh cilantro, parsley or basil

⅓ cup organic mayonnaise
⅓ cup plain yogurt
2 Tbsp. mustard of choice
1 ½ Tbsp. raw honey
1-2 tsp. curry powder
½ tsp. sea salt
¼ tsp. ground pepper

Suggested Pairings:
Red Rebel Soup (pg 71), Great Granola (pg 63), Warm Cheese and Artichoke Dip (pg 64), Harvest Bisque (pg 72).

1. In medium bowl combine the chicken, carrots, celery, raisins, green onions, cilantro, mayonnaise, yogurt, mustard, honey, curry powder, salt and pepper. Mix the ingredients together until well combined.

2. Serve the salad in a halved avocado with whole grain toasts, endive spoons, sesame crackers or on a bed of greens. ℰ

Fresh Fruit with Mascarpone Dip

Your next fresh fruit platter won't be missed with this delightful mascarpone dip.

Ingredients:

Mascarpone Dip:

8 ounces mascarpone cheese, at
   room temperature
5 Tbsp. raw honey
1 cup chilled heavy whipping cream
2 tsp. orange liquor (see pg. 10) or
   pure almond extract

Fruit:

Pineapple, cut in slim squares
Melon, cut into bite sized squares
1-2 pounds cleaned organic berries
Sliced organic apples, peaches and
   nectarines

Suggested Pairings:
Breakfast Casserole
(pg 49), Egg Salad
and Endive
(pg 62), Polenta
Lasagna (pg 88),
Holiday Ham

1. In a small bowl, cream together the mascarpone and honey.
2. In a large mixing bowl beat the heavy cream on high speed for 1-2 minutes or until stiff peaks begin to form. Reduce the mixing speed to low and add the orange liquor. Continue to beat on high speed for another 30-60 seconds. Add 1/3 of marscapone mixture to the cream mixture beat on high speed for 30 seconds. Then gradually beat in the remaining marscapone mixture into the cream mixture. Chill the dip immediately until ready to serve.
3. Arrange the prepared fruit on a large serving platter with a dish of the Mascarpone Dip. ᔆᴑ

Egg Salad and Endive

A homemade staple fashionably presented. Prepare this dish for your next brunch
or for everyday breakfast and lunch.

Ingredients:

12 hardboiled eggs, peeled and diced
⅓ cup minced dill pickle
⅓ cup organic mayonnaise
¼ cup yellow mustard
¾ tsp. sea salt
3 Tbsp. minced fresh chives

½ tsp. dried dill or 2 Tbsp.
    fresh, minced
½ tsp. ground black pepper
1-2 heads baby Belgium endive
Paprika, fresh dill, chives or shredded
    purple cabbage for garnish

1. In a large bowl, combine the eggs, pickles, salt, dill and pepper. Stir until well combined and store in the fridge until ready to serve.
2. Wash, dry and trim the baby endive leaves. Arrange the leaves on your serving platter. Place one 2 tablespoons of the prepared salad on each leaf. Garnish with fresh herbs and/or a dash of paprika and serve. ℳ

Suggested Pairings:
Fresh Fruit with
Marscapone Dip
(pg 61), Asparagus
Bisque (pg 69),
Baked Banana and
Date Bread (pg 113),
Carrot Cakes (pg 114)

Prep Time:
15 minutes

Soak Time:
6-8 hours

Slow Bake Time:
8-10 hours

Yields:
3 cups granola

Great Granola

Enjoy this nourishing treat with milk, yogurt or as a simple snack.

Ingredients:

1 ½ **cup rolled oats**
⅔ **cup walnuts or pecans**
½ **cup raisins**
2 **tsp. cinnamon**
¼ **tsp. sea salt**
½ **cup water**
4 **Tbs. butter, melted**

½ **cup pure maple syrup or agave nectar**
1 ½ **Tbs. plain yogurt or whey**

1. In a medium bowl combine the oats, nuts, raisins, cinnamon and salt. Stir in the water, maple syrup, butter and yogurt. Mix until well combined and let rest, covered, on the counter for 6-8 hours.

2. Preheat the oven on to the warm setting or around 150-170°. Line a baking sheet with parchment paper and grease it with butter or coconut oil. Spread the soaked oat mixture on the lined pan. Place it in the warmed oven for 8-10 hours or until lightly toasted. Remove the pan from the oven. Using a spatula, immediatly transfer the granola to a shallow bowl to cool. The granola will still be soft when warm and will harden as it dries. Store the cooled granola in an airtight container for up to 4 weeks. &

*Suggested Pairings:
Honey Yogurt
pg 24, Homemade
Greek Yogurt
pg 24, prepared
eggs pg 36,
BEST Salad pg 54,
Family Frittata
pg 49, fresh
fruit, milk*

Warm Cheese and Artichoke Dip

A perfect warm dip for your next gathering or a healthy fun lunch for the family.

Ingredients:

have ready at room temperature

8 ounces goat cheese or substitute cream cheese

2 Tbsp. lemon juice

3 Tbsp. olive oil

1 clove garlic, minced

¼ tsp. sea salt

¼ tsp. red pepper flakes or ground black pepper

1 5-ounce jar marinated artichokes, drained and chopped

4 ounces (½ cup) frozen chopped spinach, thawed and drained (optional)

¼ cup grated sharp Italian cheese (optional, I like to add this if I'm using cream cheese)

2 Tbsp. minced chilies (optional)

6 cups veggie crudités (carrot sticks, celery, broccoli, cauliflower, cherry tomatoes and cucumber)

1. In a medium bowl or food processor combine together the cheese, lemon juice, olive oil, garlic, salt and pepper. Stir in the artichokes, spinach and chilies.

2. Preheat the oven 400°. Place the prepared dip in a greased baking dish and bake for 15 minutes. Serve immediately with veggies crudité.

Cook's Note:
This dip can be made ahead of time and stored in the fridge for up to 6 days or frozen for up to 6 months.

Prep Time:
10 minutes

Total Soaking and
Cooking Time:
24 hours

Yields:
3 cups

Super Snack Mix

These toasty nuts and seeds are the perfect combination of salty and sweet, boosted with a super sprouted crunch! (For more info on soaking and sprouting see pg 14.)

Ingredients:

1 cup raw sunflower seeds
1 cup raw pecans or walnuts
⅔ cup raw almonds
3 cups filtered water for soaking
1 ¼ tsp. sea salt, divided
⅓ cup pure maple syrup or
    agave nectar

1 ¼ tsp. ground cinnamon
⅛ tsp. ground cayenne pepper
    (optional)
½ cup bittersweet chocolate chips
    (optional)
½ cup dried cranberries or raisins
    (optional)

*Cook's Note:
These nuts make
a great snack for
everyday or a
special event. I like
to pack them in
school lunches
and serve them as
an appetizer at
our friendly
gatherings.*

1. Place all the nuts and seeds in a large glass container with the filtered water and ½ tsp. salt. Cover with the lid and leave out at room temperature for 10-12 hours.
2. Line a baking sheet with parchment paper and grease the paper with butter or coconut oil. Pre-heat oven to 150-170 degrees or place it on the warm setting.
3. Drain and rinse the soaked nuts and gently dry them with a paper towel. In a large bowl combine the nuts, maple syrup, ¾ tsp. salt, cinnamon and cayenne. Once coated, spread the nuts on the prepared sheet pan. Place them in the oven for 10-12 hours until they are dried and slightly toasted. Remove the nuts from the oven and immediately transfer them to a large bowl and allow to cool.
4. The nuts will last up to six weeks in an air tight container at room temperature. Enjoy them as a snack, as a topping on naturally sweetened yogurt or tossed together with chocolate pieces, dried fruit if you like. ✆

Prep Time:
15 minutes

Cook time:
20 minutes

Yields:
8-10 servings

Super Nachos and Tacos

A party on a plate for the whole family to enjoy!

Ingredients:

Nacho/Taco Meat:

2 pounds ground beef or
    ground turkey
1 ¾ tsp. sea salt
¾ tsp. ground black pepper
1 Tbsp. ground cumin
1 ½ Tbsp. chili powder
2 tsp. paprika
1 tsp. garlic powder
1 Tbsp. apple cider vinegar or
    lime juice
1 14-ounce can diced tomatoes,
    drained or 1 ½ cups prepared salsa

Suggested Pairings:

Organic corn chips or tortillas
Cooked beans
Prepared Cajun Rice (pg 21)
Prepared Salsa, diced fresh tomatoes
    or Pico Di Gallo (pg 52)
Guacamole or diced avocado
Shredded Monterey jack or
    cheddar cheese
Sour cream or plain whole
    milk yogurt
Sliced black olives
Chopped green onion
Sliced fresh or pickled jalapeños

Cook's Note:
This nacho batch is naturally seasoned, so don't hesitate to keep coming back for more. By leaving the famous "taco seasoning" packet on the market shelf you are guaranteed to save a buck as well as lowering your family's sodium intake along with any other mystery ingredients.

1. Heat a medium sauce pan over medium to high heat. Add the ground meat to the hot pan, along with the salt and pepper. Brown the meat, then turn off the heat and let the fat settle for 2-3 minutes. Drain away most of the settled fat.
2. Heat the meat again on low heat and stir in the cumin, chili powder, paprika and garlic powder. Then add the vinegar and diced tomatoes; stir until well combined. Cover with a lid and let simmer for 5-10 minutes.
3. Serve the prepared meat with your favorite nacho or taco fixings. ∽

Superb Soups

Soups are so, so good. They are the perfect way to transform seasonal produce into pure comfort food. This chapter reveals some of my favorite soup recipes. Many are slow cooker friendly, vegetarian, paleo and gluten free. Enjoy these warm healthy, nourishing delights!🙵

Veggie Minestrone

A healthy dish that your whole family will enjoy! Perfect for those cold winter days when the holidays are through and a vegetarian stew seems just right.

Prep Time:
15 minutes

Cook time:
90 minutes,
stove top;
5-8 hours,
slow cooker

Yields:
8-10 servings

Ingredients:

2 Tbsp. olive oil
2 Tbsp. butter
1 ½ cup (1 large) onion, chopped
1 ½ cup celery, chopped
1 ½ cup carrots, chopped
4 cloves garlic, minced
1 ½ tsp. sea salt
½ tsp. pepper
1 ½ Tbsp. dried oregano
¼ cup tomato paste
3-4 cups water
1 bay leaf

1 sharp Italian cheese rind (optional)
1 28-ounce can diced tomatoes
1 ¾ cups cooked red kidney beans
    (1 15-ounce can, drained and
    rinsed)
1 ¾ cups cooked garbanzo beans
    (1 15-ounce can, drained and
    rinsed)
2 Tbsp. tahini (optional)
½ cup grated sharp Italian cheese
    plus additional for garnish
1 cup fresh parsley, chopped

1. Heat a large sauce pan over med heat; add the oil, butter and onion, cook for 1-2 minutes. Add the celery and carrots and cook 1-2 minutes. Add the garlic, salt, pepper, oregano and tomato paste and cook for another minute.

2. Next, stir in the water, bay leaf, cheese rind, diced tomatoes and beans to the pot. Bring to a simmer, turn the heat to low, cover and cook for 90 minutes, until the veggies are tender.

3. Once cooked, remove the bay leaf and the cheese rind. Stir in the tahini, cheese and fresh parsley. Serve with fresh grated sharp Italian cheese.

4. If using slow cooker place all the ingredients in the slow cooker except for the parsley, tahini and cheese. Cook on high for 5 hours or on low for 8 hours. Stir in the tahini, cheese and parsley before serving and garnish with grated sharp Italian cheese. 🙰

Suggested Pairings:
Fried Eggs (pg 36),
Honey Nut
Chippers (pg 110),
Garlic Toast

Prep Time:
20 minutes

Cook Time:
30 minutes

Yields:
6 servings

Asparagus Bisque

This soup is sure to please; luscious and light with deceptively rich flavor.

Ingredients:

1 pound fresh asparagus
2 Tbsp. butter
1 cup onion, chopped
¼ tsp. sea salt
¼ tsp. pepper
1 Tbsp. (3 cloves) garlic, roughly
   chopped
¼ cup dry white wine or lemon juice
4 cups chicken or vegetable broth
1 large potato, peeled and diced
   or 1 ½ cup chopped cauliflower

1 bay leaf
1 parmesan or Romano cheese rind
   (optional)
½ cup plain yogurt or sour cream
½ cup freshly grated Romano or
   parmesan cheese, plus additional
   for garnish (optional)
¼ cup fresh parsley or dill
Salt and pepper to taste

Cook's Note:
This recipe can be
used to make
Broccoli Cheddar
Bisque. Simply
substitute 1 pound
broccoli for the
asparagus and
substitute 2 cups
shredded sharp
cheddar cheese for
the Italian cheese.

1. Clean and trim the asparagus then chop into 1-inch pieces. Place the asparagus tips (about 1 cup) in a steam basket and cook for 5 minutes until tender, then set aside to cool.

2. Heat a large sauce pan over med-high heat. Add the butter, onion and salt; sauté for 2-3 minutes. Add the garlic and cook for 1 minute longer. Then add the wine or lemon juice to the pan and cook for another minute.

3. Add the remaining raw asparagus, broth, diced potato, lemon juice, bay leaf and cheese rind to the pan. Bring to a simmer, cover and cook on low for 25 minutes.

4. Remove the rind and bay leaf from the pan and add the yogurt, cheese and parsley. Using an immersion blender, puree the soup until smooth. Then stir in the parsley and steamed asparagus tips. Garnish with cheese , fresh herbs and serve.

Prep-time:
15 minutes

Cook time:
50 minutes,
stove top;
4-7 hours,
slow cooker

Yields:
6 servings

Tomato Soup Florentine

The smooth delicious texture of this soup will surely make
store-bought soup a thing of the past.

Ingredients:

2 Tbsp. olive oil
1 Tbsp. butter
1 large onion, chopped
½ tsp. sea salt
¼ tsp. ground black pepper
4 cloves garlic, chopped
1 large carrot, chopped (1 cup)
¼ cup lemon juice or white wine
1 28 ounce can crushed tomatoes
    with basil
2 cups chicken broth or water

1 sharp italian cheese rind (optional)
½ cup sour cream
2-3 cups chopped fresh Swiss chard
    or spinach leaves
½ cup shredded sharp italian cheese,
    plus additional for garnish
Salt and pepper to taste

Cook's Note:
*I like to
serve this soup with
crusty garlic bread
and/or breaded
chicken tenders. It is
also fun to turn it into
"Pizza Soup" and let
your family add their
favorite Pizza
toppings, such as
fresh basil,
mozzarella, sliced
olives and
hot peppers..*

1. Heat the oil and butter in a medium sauce pan over med-high heat, add the onion, salt and pepper; sauté for 2-3 minutes. Add the garlic and carrots, cook 1 minute longer, then add the wine or lemon juice and simmer for another 30 seconds.
2. Add the tomatoes, stock and cheese rind to the pot. Bring to a simmer, reduce heat to low, cover and cook for 40 minutes. For the slow cooker, cook for 4 hours on high heat or 7 hours on low heat.
3. Turn off the heat and remove the cheese rind. Add the sour cream and puree the soup with an immersion blender.
4. Stir in the greens and cheese. Heat the soup to desired temperature and serve plain or with your favorite toppings.

Red Rebel Soup

A collection of nature's captivating colors are in this soup, beautiful hues of orange, red and purple will warm your body into the depths of nourishment.

Ingredients:

½ cup dry red lentils, quinoa or
   1 ¾ cup (1 16-ounce can) cooked
   garbanzo beans, rinsed and
   drained
1 tsp. sea salt, divided
2 Tbsp. coconut oil or ghee
1 medium onion, chopped
½ cup celery, chopped
1 red bell pepper, diced
¾ cup carrot, diced
¾ cup (1 med.) beet, diced
1 ½ cup (1 medium) yam, peeled
   and diced

3 cloves garlic, minced
1 Tbsp. dry basil (optional)
 1 tsp. paprika
½ tsp. ground cinnamon
⅛ tsp. ground cayenne or a minced
   habanero chili (optional)
4 cups vegetable or chicken broth
4 cups water
1 cup fresh cilantro, chopped
2 Tbsp. apple cider vinegar or fresh
   lime juice

Pre-Soaking
and Prep Time:
8-10 hrs.

Prep time:
15 minutes

Cook time:
50 minutes,
stove top;
4-8 hours,
slow cooker

Yields:
8-10 servings

*Suggested
Pairings:*
*Fresh corn, Fried
Eggs (pg 36),
Curry Chicken
Salad (pg 60),
Sesame Tandoori
Chicken (pg 102),
Coconut Lime
Truffles (pg 112)*

1. Place the lentils or quinoa in small bowl on the counter with 1 cup filtered water and ¼ tsp. sea salt. Cover and let them set out on the counter for 8-10 hours. Drain and rinse them before using.
2. Heat a large sauce pan over medium heat, add the ghee or oil, onion, celery, pepper and salt to the pan, sauté for 2-3 minutes. Add the carrot, beet, yam, garlic, basil, paprika, cinnamon and cayenne and cook for an additional 1 minute.
3. Add the broth, water, bay leaf and lentils or quinoa to the pan and bring to a simmer. Reduce the heat to low, cover and simmer for 50-60 minutes or until the veggies are tender. For the slow cooker, cook on high for 4 hours or low for 8 hours.
4. Stir in the fresh cilantro and vinegar and more salt and spice to taste. ℘

Prep Time:
30 minutes

Cook Time:
1 hour 30 min.,
stove top;
4-6 hours,
slow cooker

Yields:
12 servings

Harvest Bisque

This soothing bisque hits the spot when the air is brisk outside and the ailments of the cold season begin to nip. The slightly sweet, curried flavors will be savored with every sip.

Ingredients:

1 large butternut squash or pumpkin
   (2-3 pounds)
1 large onion, peeled and cut
   in quarters
2 carrots, roughly chopped
2 large apples, peeled and sliced in
   large pieces (away from the core)
1 yam, peeled and cut into quarters
   (or substitute additional carrots)
12 ounces uncooked bacon, chopped
2 Tbsp. fresh ginger, peeled and
   chopped or 1 ½ tsp. ground ginger
3 cloves garlic, roughly chopped
1 ½ tsp. sea salt
1 Tbsp. curry powder
1 ½ tsp. ground cumin

1 tsp. dried thyme
1 tsp. ground cinnamon
½ tsp. ground black pepper
¼ tsp. ground cayenne pepper
   (optional)
3-4 cups water
1 14-ounce can coconut milk
3 Tbsp. raw honey or pure maple
   syrup
Plain whole milk yogurt or
   sour cream (garnish)
Chopped cooked bacon or
   toasted pumpkin seeds (garnish)
Dash of hot sauce (garnish)

Suggested pairings:
BEST Salad (pg 54),
Super Snack Mix
(pg 65), Roasted
Brussels Sprouts
(pg 85), Sesame
Tandoori Chicken
(pg 102), Baked
Banana Date Bread
(pg 113)

1. Preheat the oven 375°. Grease the bottom of a large roasting pan or baking dish with coconut oil or olive oil.
2. Cut the squash in half lengthwise and remove the seeds. Place it in the roasting dish along with the onion, carrots, apples and yam. Loosely cover the pan, place it in the heated oven and roast for 1 hour or until just tender, then cool.
3. Meanwhile, in a large sauce pan, cook the bacon over medium heat. Transfer the cooked bacon pieces to a dish lined with a paper towel; reserve 2 Tbsp. of the bacon grease in the bottom of the pan. Add the ginger, garlic, salt, curry powder, cumin, cinnamon and pepper to the pan with the bacon grease and cook over medium heat for 1-2 minutes.
4. Remove the flesh of the roasted butternut squash with a large spoon and add it to the pan with the sautéed herbs and spices, along with the other roasted veggies and fruits. Cover the veggies with water, bring to a boil, and then reduce the heat to low. Cover and simmer for 45 minutes on the stove or use the slow cooker for 5 hours on low or 3 hours on high.
5. Using an immersion blender puree the soup until smooth. Then stir in the coconut milk, honey, salt and pepper to taste. Serve, garnished with a dollop of plain yogurt, chopped bacon pieces and a dash of your favorite hot sauce.

Cook's Note:
If you'd like to prepare this soup vegetarian-style then simply substitute 2 Tbsp. coconut oil or butter for the bacon grease, and add 1 ½ tsp. smoked paprika. Garnish with toasted pumpkin seeds or toasted coconut.

Vanessa's Kitchen - Pure Food Joy!

Sensational Salads and Sides

This chapter debuts some of my favorite, pure food recipes. A bursting bouquet of vegetable, grain, fruit and legume dishes seasoned with nourishing dressings and packed with the punch of Super Food Power! Keep a stock in the fridge for a healthy lunch during the week or pair them with your favorite *Simple Protein* (pg 33) for fast everyday meals. The gourmet flavors will make a statement at any gathering, large or small.∞

Prep Time:
15 minutes

Yields:
6-8 servings

Asian Sesame Slaw

Sweet and tangy with a hint of toasted sesame, this tasty slaw will satisfy that Asian noodle craving.

Ingredients:

½ cup apple cider vinegar

⅓ cup organic whole fruit apricot preserves or ¼ cup raw honey

1 tsp. ground ginger or 1 Tbsp. minced fresh ginger

1 tsp. sea salt

½ tsp. red pepper flakes (optional)

1 Tbsp. toasted sesame oil

6 cups shredded cabbage (napa or green)

1 ½ cups carrots, shredded

1 cup red bell pepper, thinly sliced

½ cup scallions or chives, chopped

¾ cup fresh cilantro, chopped

1 tbsp. toasted sesame seeds, preferably unhulled (optional)

1. In a large bowl whisk together the vinegar, preserves, ginger, sea salt, pepper and sesame oil.
2. To toast sesame seeds, heat a cast iron skillet over medium heat, place the seeds in the pan and toast for 1-2 minutes.
3. Add the cabbage, carrots, red pepper, scallions, cilantro and sesame seeds. Toss all ingredients together and let the slaw marinate for 1-2 hours before serving. ℰ🝆

Cook's Note: For a complete meal, double the dressing recipe following step #1. Warm the extra dressing in a sauce pan and use it to top cooked chicken, fish or shrimp. Serve with prepared brown rice and the Asian Sesame Slaw.

Prep Time:
15 minutes

Yields:
4-6 servings

Super Broccoli Salad

This dish features raw broccoli at its best! Enjoy it as a side or pack it for a quick lunch on the go.

Ingredients:

3 Tbsp. sour cream or plain whole milk yogurt

⅓ cup apple cider vinegar

3 Tbsp. raw honey

1 tsp. sea salt

¼ tsp. black or ground cayenne pepper

2 Tbsp. mayonnaise or olive oil

3 ½ cups broccoli, chopped

1 cup shredded purple cabbage, purple kohlrabi and/or shredded carrots

3 Tbsp. onion, chopped

⅔ cup red grapes, cut in half, or ¼ cup raisins

¼ cup chopped cooked bacon or super toasty sunflower seeds (see pg 15)

¼ cup blue cheese crumbles (optional)

Suggested Pairings: Steak or Lamb Chops (pg 43), Classic Roast Chicken (pg 29), Irish Stew with Soda Bread (pg 90), Carrot Cakes (pg 114)

1. In a medium bowl whisk together the sour cream, vinegar, honey, salt and pepper. Then whisk in the mayonnaise.
2. Toss in the broccoli, cabbage, onion, grapes or raisins, bacon and blue cheese. Store in the fridge for at least 4 hours prior to serving. ℘

Preparation
Time:
15 minutes

Roast Time:
30-40 minutes

Yields:
6-8 servings

Curry Roasted Cauliflower and Sweet Onion

This is a flavorful dish that can be enjoyed both warm and cold. It is a perfect side to any Asian inspired dish and can also be enhanced with fresh greens and toasty nuts for a vegetarian feast.

*Cook's Note:
If you don't care
for onion, simply
omit it and reduce
the salt to ¾ tsp
and the coconut
oil to 1 Tbsp.*

Ingredients:

1 Tbsp. butter or ghee
2 Tbsp. coconut oil
1 tsp. sea salt
1 ½ tsp. curry powder
1 small head cauliflower, chopped
  (4-5 cups)
2 cups sliced sweet onion

2 cups fresh baby spinach (optional)
Fresh cilantro (optional)
Fresh lime juice (optional)
Favorite hot sauce (optional garnish)
Toasted pumpkin seeds or cashews
  (optional garnish)

1. Preheat the oven 400°. In a small sauce pan, melt together the butter, coconut oil, salt and curry powder.
2. Place the cauliflower and onion in a large bowl, pour over the melted coconut oil mixture and toss until coated. Spread the cauliflower and onion on a large baking sheet. Place in the heated oven and roast for 30-40 minutes until golden and tender.
3. Transfer the warm cauliflower to a serving bowl and toss in the fresh spinach, lime juice, cilantro and garnishes before serving. ℘

Prep Time:
20 minutes

Cook Time:
5 minutes

Yields:
6 servings

Black Bean, Corn and Avocado Salad

This dish is a sure crowd pleaser!

Ingredients:

Dressing:

1 clove garlic

1 tsp. sea salt

1 habanero pepper, seeded and minced (optional for heat)

3 Tbsp. lime juice, 1-2 limes

2 Tbsp. apple cider

½ tsp. chili powder

½ tsp. ground cumin

2 Tbsp. olive oil

Salad:

½ cup red onion, finely diced

1 cup fresh or frozen corn, thawed

1 cup diced orange bell pepper

1 15-ounce can black beans, rinsed and drained (1 ¾ cup cooked beans)

2 roma tomatoes, seeded and diced

1 small avocado, diced

1 cup fresh cilantro, minced

Suggested Pairings:
Grilled Cajun Chicken Drummies (pg 42), Fruit Smoothie (pg 56), Blackened Mahi Mahi with Blueberry Slaw (pg 94) Coconut Lime Truffles (pg 112)

1. First prepare the dressing. Smash the garlic clove with a large knife on a cutting board, sprinkle it with salt and mince it into a paste. Place the paste in a small container, with the minced habanero, and whisk in the lime juice, vinegar, chili powder, cumin and olive oil and set aside.

2. Heat a large cast iron skillet or a heavy bottomed skillet. In the dry, hot pan, sauté the onion, corn and peppers over medium-high heat for 3-5 minutes or until lightly browned. Transfer the ingredients to a medium bowl and stir in the black beans. (This can be done ahead of time.)

3. Just before serving toss diced tomato with the bean mixture, the dressing, avocado and cilantro. Serve immediately with greens, tortilla chips or your favorite prepared meats or fish.

Prep Time:
25 minutes

Cook Time:
50 minutes

Yields:
6-8 servings

Coconut Rice Salad with Cilantro-Lime Vinaigrette

A delicious and refreshing dish that makes the perfect summer side dish or meal.

Ingredients:

Coconut Curry Rice:

1 cup brown rice

1 cup water

1 Tbsp. whey or plain yogurt (optional)

1 tsp. sea salt divided

1 13.5 ounce can coconut milk

1 tsp. curry powder

Cilantro Lime Vinaigrette:

½ cup lime juice (2-3 limes)

¼ cup apple cider vinegar

2 Tbsp. raw unfiltered honey

¼ cup olive oil

2 cups cup fresh cilantro

2 green onions

1 fresh jalapeño pepper, seeded (optional)

1 1-inch piece fresh ginger, peeled or ½ tsp. ground ginger

1 tsp. sea salt

Salad:

choose a few or all of these ingredients to make a beautiful meal

4-6 cups mixed greens or baby spinach

1 cup cucumber, sliced

1 cup purple cabbage shredded

1 cup sliced red bell pepper

1-2 cups fresh mango slices

⅓ cup toasted cashews or toasted coconut flakes

Cook's Note: I sometimes double the recipe for Cilantro-Lime Vinaigrette and use it to coat chicken breast for a Cilantro-Lime Chicken.

1. Rinse the rice and soak it overnight prior to cooking. To do this, combine the rice, water, whey and salt in a medium sauce pan, cover with a lid and let rest at room temperature for 8-14 hours. This is an optional step, but it can enhance the nutrients and texture of the rice (see pg 19).
2. When ready to cook the rice, stir in the coconut milk, and curry powder. Bring to a simmer, reduce the heat to low, cover and cook for 40 minutes. Remove the pan from the heat and allow it to rest for 10 minutes.
3. Meanwhile, prepare the *Cilantro Lime Vinaigrette*. Using a blender or food processor, combine the lime juice, vinegar, honey, olive oil, cilantro, onions, jalaeño, ginger and sea salt; puree for 1 minute.
4. Mix half of the prepared vinaigrette into the cooled rice. In a large bowl combine the greens, shredded cabbage or cucumber. Drizzle with the remaining dressing and toss together. Place the rice on top of the dressed veggies. Garnish with red pepper and mango slices; top with cashews and/or large toasted coconut flakes.

Suggested Pairings:

Chicken Tenders (pg 41), Sesame Tandoori Chicken (pg 102), Zucchini Brownies a la mode (pg 122)

Prep Time:
25 minutes

Rest Time:
6-12 hours

Yields:
12 serving

Lemon Veggie Quinoa Salad

This recipe is a summertime favorite! It disappears fast at every picnic party.
A wonderful whole grain substitute for pasta salad.

Ingredients:

Lemon Herb Dressing:

2-3 lemons juiced (½ cup lemon juice)
1 clove garlic, 1 tsp minced
⅓ cup fresh parsley
1 tsp sea salt
½ tsp ground black pepper
½ tsp dried thyme or 1 Tbsp.
   fresh thyme
¼ cup olive oil

Salad Ingredients:

1 15-ounce can (1 ¾ cup) cooked
   garbanzo beans, drained and
   rinsed
¾ cup dry quinoa
½ cups water
¼ tsp. sea salt
2 cups (1 pound) chopped asparagus
   or zucchini
2 tsp. butter
½ tsp. sea salt
2 cups baby spinach or arugula leaves
1 cup sliced red pepper or cherry
   tomatoes, sliced in half
½ cup sharp Italian cheese cut into
   small cubes or feta crumbles
½ cup fresh basil, torn (optional)
3 Tbsp. minced red or green onion

*Cook's Note:
The Lemon Herb
Dressing is a
wonderful
dressing marinade
for chicken, too.
I will sometimes
prepare a second
batch to dress
grilled chicken.*

1. Using a blender or food processor, prepare the *Lemon Herb Dressing*. Blend together the lemon juice, garlic, parsley, salt, pepper, thyme and olive oil.
2. In a container, combine the garbanzo beans and prepared dressing, cover and chill for 6-12 hours. The quinoa can also be soaked ahead of time for 6-10 hours (see pg. 19).
3. Prepare the quinoa. Using a colander rinse the quinoa. In a small sauce pan, combine the quinoa, water and ¼ tsp. salt. Bring the mixture to a simmer over med-high heat. Reduce heat to low, cover and cook for 15-20 minutes. Remove the pan from heat, let it rest for 5 minutes then fluff with a fork. Cool completely until ready to assemble the salad.
4. Heat a large skillet over med- high heat. Melt the butter in the pan, then asparagus and ½ tsp. salt. Sauté over med to med-high heat for 5-7 minutes, until just tender.
5. In large bowl combine the cooked quinoa, garbanzo beans with the dressing, the spinach, red pepper, cheese, basil and onion. Toss well, garnish with fresh herbs and serve.

Suggested Pairings:
Chicken Tenders (pg 41), Honey Yogurt (pg 24)
Fresh Fruit and Mascarpone Dip (pg 61), Apricot Ricotta Cheesecake with Fruit (pg 120)

Prep Time:
15 minutes

Yields:
4-6 servings

Kale Chopped Salad

This salad pairs wonderfully with pork, beef, or lamb. It is a pleasant surprise to see how much this elegant and healthy salad is enjoyed by all ages.

Ingredients:

3 Tbsp. plain yogurt or sour cream

3 Tbsp. spicy brown or whole grain mustard

⅓ cup + 1 Tbsp. apple cider vinegar

2 Tbsp. raw honey

1 tsp. sea salt

⅛ tsp. ground pepper

2-3 Tbsp. organic mayonnaise or olive oil

1 small apple, sliced away from the core and diced

¼ cup raisins

1 carrot, shredded

¾ cup shredded purple cabbage, beet or additional carrot

3 Tbsp. onion, chopped

6 cups chopped kale

½ cup shredded sharp cheddar cheese or crumbled blue cheese

Suggested Pairings:
Steak or Lamb Chops (pg 43), Classic Roast Chicken (pg 29), Pan Fried Pork with Apple Glaze (pg 45), Apple Butternut Muffins (pg 125)

1. In a large bowl whisk together the yogurt, mustard, vinegar, honey, salt, pepper and mayonnaise.

2. Add apple, raisins, carrot, cabbage, onion, kale and cheese to the bowl with the dressing. Toss everything together and store for 6-12 hours in the fridge before serving.

Prep Time:
10 minutes

Bake Time:
35-40 minutes

Yields:
4 servings

Roasted Brussels Sprouts

Brussels sprouts have grown on me over time. Sometimes I can't get enough of these mouth-popping morsels. I like to eat them plain or add them to a salad dressed with balsamic vinegar.

Ingredients:

1 pound Brussels sprouts

5 cloves garlic, peeled and roughly chopped or 1 large shallot peeled and sliced

¾ tsp sea salt

½ tsp. ground pepper

3 Tbsp. olive oil or melted ghee

¼ cup dried cranberries (optional)

Almond slivers or chopped cooked bacon (optional)

1. Preheat the oven 375°. Clean and trim the Brussels sprouts, if they are large, cut them in half.

2. In a large bowl, toss together the Brussels sprouts, garlic or shallot, salt, pepper and olive oil. Spread them in a large baking sheet, cover with foil, and bake for 25 minutes. Uncover the sprouts and roast for an additional 15-20 minutes until browned, crispy and tender. Toss with dried cranberries and almond slivers or bacon, if you like, before serving.

Suggested Pairings:
Pan Fried Pork with Apple Glaze (pg 45), Pecan Crusted Pork Tenderloin with Pear Cream Sauce (pg 106), Pecan Pumpkin Pie with Maple Whip (pg 126)

Vanessa's Kitchen - Pure Food Joy!

Fabulous Feasts

These recipes are a compilation of my favorite meals. Such a variety of great flavors, highlighting each season, that will satisfy your guests, family and friends. There are more salad and side dishes provided in this chapter that pair perfectly with the suggested main course and will also do well on their own. Enjoy!

Polenta Lasagna with Everyday Italian Salad

A yummy feast fit for a crew!

Ingredients:

Sauce:
1 pound Italian Sausage, cooked
2 ½ cups (1 24-ounce jar) prepared marinara sauce

Ricotta Filling:
1 ½ cup ricotta cheese
2 ½ cup grated mozzarella cheese

Crust:
2 Tbs. olive oil
4 Tbs. butter
1 Tbs. garlic, minced
4 cups filtered water
1 tsp. sea salt
2 tsp. oregano

2 cup course ground cornmeal (grits)
1 ½ cup grated Parmesan cheese, divided
1 cup frozen chopped organic spinach, thawed and drained (optional)
1 ½ Tbsp. (3 cloves) garlic, minced
½ tsp. sea salt or more to taste
¼ tsp. ground black pepper

Toppings:
1 ½ cup grated whole milk mozzarella cheese
Additional marinara sauce

Cook's Note:
If preparing Vegetarian Polenta Lasagna. Then substitute an additional 1 cup marinara sauce for the Italian sausage.

1. First combine the cooked sausage and marinara sauce and set aside.
2. Then prepare the filling by mixing the ricotta, mozzarella, spinach, garlic, salt and pepper in a medium bowl and set aside.
3. Preheat the oven 375°. Grease a 13x9 inch baking dish with olive oil.
4. Next prepare the polenta crust. Heat the oil, butter and garlic in a medium, heavy bottomed sauce pan over medium heat for 1 minute. Then add water, salt and oregano. Bring to a simmer and whisk in the cornmeal. Reduce heat to low and

continue to whisk and simmer until the mixture becomes thickened and the corn meal is tender, about 10-15 minutes. Remove pan from heat and stir in the parmesan cheese. Immediately pour half of the polenta into the baking dish. Use a rubber spatula to press the polenta into a thin layer over the bottom and up the edges of the pan. Place the pan in the heated oven and bake for 8 minutes until firm. Cover the remaining polenta until ready to use.

5. Top the bottom crust with half of the sauce. Add dollops of the ricotta filling and gently spread. Using a rubber spatula gently spread the remaining polenta over the cheese filling.

6. Place the pan in the oven and bake for 20 minutes to set the polenta. Spread the remaining sauce over the top, along with the grated mozzarella cheese and any other toppings of choice. Continue to bake for an additional 35-40 minutes. Allow the lasagna to rest for 5 minutes before serving. ∞

Prep Time:
15 minutes

Rest Time:
1-4 hours

Yields:
10 servings

Everyday Italian Salad

This yummy salad will be enjoyed by all ages. It was a staple at my family dinners growing up. At the age of 10 I took on making this nightly dish, a task that I loved to do.

Suggested Pairings:
Fresh Fruit with
Marscapone Dip
(pg 61), Chocolate
Raspberry Torte
(pg 118)

Ingredients:

Salad:

2 ½ cups of your favorite salad veggies, cleaned and sliced (tomato, cucumber, bell pepper, celery, carrot, radish)

3-4 Tbsp. diced onion

1 clove garlic, minced

1 tsp. sea salt

¼ tsp. ground black pepper

2 tsp. dried oregano

⅓ cup green Spanish olives plus 2 Tbsp. of the olive brine

⅔ cup apple cider vinegar

¼ cup olive oil

8-10 cups leaf lettuce, cleaned and chopped

Optional Toppings:

½ cup diced provolone, mozzarella or crumbled feta or blue cheese

¼ cup diced salami or pepperoni

1. Place your veggies of choice in a large salad bowl along with the onion and garlic. Season them with the salt, pepper and oregano. Add the olives, the brine, vinegar and olive oil and toss together. Cover and let marinade at room temperature for up to 4 hours.

2. Place the cleaned and trimmed lettuce on top of the marinating veggies. Toss the salad together just before meal time. Add you favorite topping and serve. ∞

Prep Time:
30 minutes

Cook Time:
2-3 hours, stove top; 4-7 hours in the slow cooker

Yields:
4-6 servings

Irish Stew and Soda Bread

Mmmmm…a warm and tasty dish that many will enjoy. Irish flavors come together for an easy, complete meal for your family and a perfect dish for entertaining guests, too.

*Suggested Pairings:
Kale Chips (pg 59),
Strawberry
Spinach Salad
(pg 93) Kale
Chop Salad
(pg 84), Super
Broccoli
Salad (pg 77).*

Ingredients:

4 Tbsp. butter or ghee
4 cups sliced onion (about 2 large)
1 Tbsp. minced garlic
1 Tbsp. natural brown sugar
1 ½ tsp. dried thyme
2 lbs. beef, lamb or venison, cubed
1 ½ tsp. sea salt
½ tsp. ground black or red pepper
½ tsp. garlic powder
½ cup dry red wine

¼ cup tomato paste
2 cups filtered water
1 ½ cup sliced carrots
1 ½ cup diced red potatoes or parsnips
2 Tbsp. arrowroot powder, tapioca flour or all-purpose flour
Irish cheddar cheese and/or sour cream for garnish

1. Heat a large sauce pan over medium heat. Add the butter, onions, brown sugar and thyme to the pan, slowly sauté until golden brown, about 7 minutes. Add the garlic and cook for 1-2 minutes longer.
2. Meanwhile, in a large bowl, combine the salt, pepper and garlic powder. Add the meat to the bowl and toss in the salt and spices until coated.
3. Heat a large skillet over medium-high heat, add the seasoned meat and brown on all sides. Then add the wine and tomato paste; simmer for 3-5 minutes.
4. Transfer the meat mixture to the large sauce pan with onions. Add the water, carrots and potato to the pan. Bring to a simmer, cover and cook for 2-3 hours on the stove or place everything in the slow cooker for 4 hours high or 7 hours low.
5. Serve the stew with grated cheese, sour cream and bread. ∞

Prep Time:
15 minutes

Rest Time:
4-8 hours

Bake Time:
35-40 minutes

Soda Bread

This yummy bread tastes great with a slather of Irish butter!

Ingredients:

1 ½ cup all-purpose flour

1 cup whole grain spelt flour or whole
    wheat flour

2 tsp. baking powder

2 tsp. baking soda

½ tsp. sea salt

1 ½ tsp. caraway seeds, optional

½ cup raisins

3 Tbsp. butter

⅓ cup honey

1 Tbsp. molasses

1 Tbsp. apple cider vinegar

1 large egg

8 ounces (1 cup) room temperature
    Irish stout beer

*Cook's Note:
Plan ahead and let
the batter rest for 2-3
hours prior to
baking the bread.
This helps to soften
the grain and
improve texture
and flavor of the
bread.*

1. In a large bowl combine together the flours, baking powder, baking soda, sea salt, caraway seeds and raisins.

2. Melt the butter in a medium sauce pan. Once melted, remove the pan from the heat and stir in the honey, molasses, vinegar, egg and beer. Gradually pour the beer mixture into the flour mixture, whisking continuously, until the batter is gooey and well combined.

3. Preheat the oven 350°. Grease and flour a standard size loaf pan. Immediately transfer the batter into the prepared pan. Place in the heated oven and bake for 35-40 minutes or until a tooth pick comes out clean. ℘

Prep time:
15 minutes

Cook Time:
15 minutes

Yields:
4 servings

Apricot–Glazed Chops and Carrots with Strawberry Spinach Salad and Lemon Poppy Seed Vinaigrette

These tangy, sweet chops are so easy to prepare, a kiddie favorite for sure. For an adult twist add chopped chipotle peppers to the apricot glaze, yum!

Cook's Note: The apricot glaze in this recipe also pairs well with grilled chicken, salmon and shrimp.

Ingredients:

2 lb. pork chops
4 cups carrots, sliced in 1/4 inch thick strips
1 Tbsp. coconut oil, ghee or butter
½ tsp. sea salt

Apricot Glaze:
½ cup whole fruit organic apricot preserves
2 ½ Tbsp. mustard or 2 Tbsp. apple cider vinegar
1-2 minced chipotle peppers (optional)

1. Since this is a quick dinner, have all the ingredients prepped before cooking begins. In a small bowl, prepare the apricot glaze by combining the preserves, mustard and chipotle peppers; set aside.
2. To cook the carrots, heat a medium skillet on the stove. Once heated, melt the coconut oil and then add the carrots and salt; sauté 3-5 minutes until just tender. Coat the carrots with the ¼ cup glaze and cook one minute longer.
3. Meanwhile, preheat a large, heavy-bottomed skillet over high heat. Season the pork chops with salt, pepper and garlic powder. Reduce heat to med-high and place the chops in the skillet. Cover with a lid and cook for about 3-4 minutes on each side until just cooked; they will be firm to the touch. Pour half of the glaze over the hot chops and let them rest in the pan for 1-2 minutes prior to serving. ℘

Strawberry Spinach Salad with Lemon Poppy Seed Vinaigrette

Summer's strawberries accented with a zesty, sweet citrus dressing is a classic pairing.

Prep Time:
15 minutes

Yields:
6 servings

Ingredients:

Lemon Poppy Seed Vinaigrette:

- 3 Tbsp. apple cider vinegar
- 2-3 Tbsp. fresh lemon juice
- 2 Tbsp. raw honey
- 1 tsp. poppy seeds
- 1 tsp. sea salt
- ¼ tsp. ground black pepper
- 2 Tbsp. sour cream or plain whole milk yogurt
- 2 Tbsp. olive oil

Salad:

- 1 ½ cup organic strawberries, sliced
- 1 carrot, cut into matchsticks
- 2 Tbsp. green onion, chopped (optional)
- 5 ounces (8 cups) baby spinach leaves
- ¼ cup super-toasty pecans (pg 15) (optional)

1. To make the **Lemon Poppy Seed Vinaigrette** whisk together the vinegar, lemon juice, honey, poppy seeds, salt, pepper, sour cream and olive oil.
2. Place the dressing along with the strawberries, carrot and onion in a large bowl. Let the mixture rest for 20-30 minutes to marinate. Then toss in the spinach and garnish with pecans 10 minutes before serving.

Suggested Pairings:
Brown Rice (pg 19), Chicken Tenders (pg 41), Super Snack Mix (pg 65), Zucchini Fudge Brownies (pg 122), Carrot Cakes (pg 114), Fruit Crisp (pg 123).

Prep Time:
20 minutes

Cook Time:
15 minutes

Yields:
6 servings

Grilled Mahi Mahi with Pineapple, Blueberry Slaw and Yummy Yam Fries

Debut the tastes of the season with this light and delicious dish.

Suggested Pairings:
Black Bean Corn and Avocado Salad (pg 79), Cajun Rice (pg 21), Coconut Lime Truffles (pg 112)

Ingredients:

Pineapple Blueberry Slaw

3 Tbsp. apple cider vinegar

3 Tbsp. lime juice (1-2 limes)

2 Tbsp. raw honey

2 Tbsp. sour cream

2 cups fresh pineapple, diced

2 cup shredded jicama and/or purple cabbage

1 cup fresh organic blueberries

½ cup diced red pepper

1 habanero chili pepper, seeded and finely chopped (optional)

½ cup Mandarin oranges, diced mango or nectarine

1 cup fresh mint or cilantro or a blend, minced

Blackened Mahi Mahi

2 lb. Mahi Mahi fillet

1 tsp. sea salt

2 tsp. chili powder

1 tsp. garlic powder

½ tsp red or black pepper

Oil for grilling

1. First, make the *Pineapple Blueberry Slaw.* In a medium bowl, whisk together the vinegar, lime juice, honey, and sour cream until smooth. Then toss in the pineapple, jicama, blueberries, peppers and red pepper and habanero. Let these ingredients marinate for 4-6 hours and then toss in the oranges, cilantro and/or mint just before serving.

2. Preheat the grill to med-high, about 400 degrees. Place the Mahi Mahi on a platter. In a small bowl combine the sea salt, chili powder, garlic powder and pepper. Rub the spice mixture over the top of the Mahi Mahi.

4. Brush the heated grill with oil. Grill the mahi mahi for 5-7 minutes and then flip and grill an additional 3-5 minutes until cooked though. Remove and serve with the prepared slaw. 🙰

Yummy Yam Fries
The perfect sweet side for everyday dinners and holiday feasts too!

Ingredients:

2 Tbsp. butter or coconut oil

¼ cup orange juice

3 Tbsp. pure maple syrup or agave nectar

1 tsp. ground cinnamon

¾ tsp. sea salt

½ tsp. cayenne or black pepper

1 ½ lbs. (3 cups) yams peeled and sliced in ½ inch wedges

¼ cup toasted coconut (pg 15) and/or pumpkin seeds (optional)

1. In a large sauce pan melt the butter, remove from the heat and then whisk in the orange juice, maple syrup, cinnamon, salt and pepper. Toss in the sliced yams and marinate for 1-6 hours (room temperature is fine) before roasting.

2. Preheat the oven to 400°. Rub a large baking sheet with coconut or olive oil. Using a slotted spoon remove the yams from the marinade (reserve the marinade), spread the yams evenly on the pan. Bake in the heated oven for 30-35 minutes or until tender.

3. Meanwhile place the reserved marinade in a small sauce pan and simmer until reduced by one third.

4. In a serving bowl toss the yams with the marinade reduction, garnish with toasted coconut or pumpkin seeds and serve. 🙰

Prep Time:
15 minutes

Rest Time:
1-6 hours

Bake Time:
30-40 minutes

Yields:
6 servings

Cook's Note:
If doubling the recipe then use two baking sheets to prevent overcrowding.

Prep Time:
25 minutes

Marinate Time:
6-20 hours

Cook Time:
15 minutes

Yields:
10 servings

Grilled Orange Balsamic Chicken with Grapes and Rosemary Roasted Potatoes

A lean and healthy dish that is bursting with flavor! A lovely all-in-one dish for your next summertime frolic with friends.

Suggested Pairings:
Warm Cheese and Artichoke
Dip (pg 64),
Blackberry Cheese
Squares (pg 124)
Chocolate Raspberry
Torte (pg 118)

Ingredients:

4 lbs. boneless skinless chicken breast, cut in half, or chicken tenders
½ cup balsamic vinegar
½ cup orange juice
¼ cup plain whole milk yogurt
2 Tbsp. olive oil
4 cloves garlic
2 tsp. sea salt

1 tsp. ground black pepper
¼ cup fresh rosemary or 1 Tbsp. dried
2 lbs. red grape bunches, cleaned, and 1 ½ cups removed from the stem
8-10 cups baby spinach
Shaved Romano or Gorgonzola crumbles (optional)
Shaved fresh fennel (optional)

1. Clean the chicken and place it in a large storage container.
2. Prepare the marinade. Combine the vinegar, orange juice, yogurt, olive oil, garlic, salt, pepper and rosemary in a blender and puree. Pour the marinade over the chicken, toss to coat. Store the chicken in the fridge for 8-24 hours.
3. Preheat the grill over medium-high heat. Place the grape bunches on the grill, turn every couple of minutes for approximately 10 minutes.
4. Remove the chicken from the marinade and transfer the marinade to a small saucepan. Add the 1 ½ cups of loose grapes and simmer on the stove top over med-low heat for 5-10 minutes until reduced by half and the grapes burst. Meanwhile, grill the chicken until cooked through.

5. Arrange the greens on a large platter and top with the prepared Rosemary Roasted Potatoes, the grilled chicken, grapes and marinade reduction. Garnish with a bunch of grilled grapes, sliced orange, rosemary leaves, cheese and fresh fennel.

Rosemary Roasted Potatoes

An easy oven home fry. The perfect accompaniment for many meals served at any time of day!

4 cups organic potatoes, cleaned and diced (1 .5 pounds, about 3 medium)
2 Tbsp. olive oil
1 tsp. sea salt

1/4 tsp. ground black pepper
1/4 tsp. garlic powder
1 Tbsp. fresh rosemary, minced or 1 tsp. dried

Ingredients:

1. Preheat the oven to 375°.
2. In a medium bowl, toss together the potatoes, olive oil, salt, pepper, garlic powder and rosemary. Spread them on a sheet pan and bake for 45 minutes, until golden brown.

Prep Time:
10 minutes

Bake Time:
45 minutes

Yields:
3-4 servings

Cook's Note:
If you are using russet potatoes, be sure to peel them before dicing them. Red and gold potatoes can be enjoyed with their skin on, just be sure to scrub them well.

Prep Time:
30 minutes

Cook Time:
2 hours, stove top;
3 hours high,
5 hours low,
slow cooker

Yields:
12-15 servings

Classic Chili with Winter Squash Cups

Chili night is a favorite night for all of my crew. There are so many ways to prepare this complete and healthy meal. Prepare it with meat or just veggies, spicy or mild. Chili is a crock-pot creation that will make your taste buds go wild!

Ingredients:

2 pounds ground beef
1 ½ tsp. sea salt
½ tsp. ground black pepper
1 ½ Tbsp. ground cumin
2 tsp. hot or mild chili powder
2 tsp. dried oregano
6 cloves garlic, minced or
   1 Tbsp. garlic powder
1 large onion, diced
1 large green bell pepper, diced

1 large carrot, diced
1 jalapeño chili, minced, optional
1 28 ounce can crushed tomatoes
1 28 ounce can diced tomatoes or
   prepared salsa
1 15 ounce can red or black beans,
   drained and rinsed
1 cup frozen corn or diced yellow
   summer squash

*Cook's Note:
For a **Vegetarian
Chili** substitute 1 15
ounce can garbanzo
beans along with 1 ½
cup diced zucchini
and 3 Tbsp. olive
oil or ghee for the
ground beef.*

1. In a large sauce pan, brown the meat over med-high heat. While it is cooking, add the salt, pepper, cumin, chili powder, oregano and garlic. Once the meat is mostly browned, add the onion, peppers and carrot to the pot and continue to cook over medium heat for 3-5 minutes.

2. Next, add the crushed and diced tomatoes, beans and corn. Bring the mixture to a simmer, cover and cook on the stove for 1 hour 45 minutes or transfer to a slow cooker and cook on low heat for 5 hours or on high heat for 3 hours.

3. Serve the chili garnished with shredded cheese, sour cream or plain yogurt and minced onions and jalapeños.

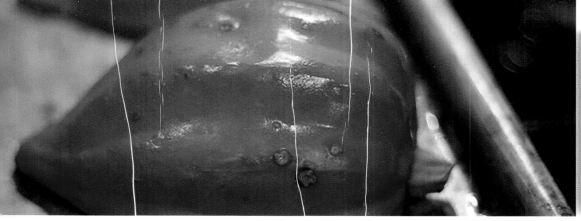

Prep Time:
5-10 minutes

Bake Time:
45-50 minutes

Yields:
4-8 servings

Winter Squash Cups

The warm, suttle sweetness of a roasted, golden squash is a natural delight.
Enjoy these simply dressed with butter and balsamic, or scoop out the roasted squash and
make a yummy puree or use them for your next chili bowl.

Ingredients:

**2 acorn, carnival, spaghetti or
    delcata squash**
Olive oil or coconut oil
Butter

Premium balsamic vinegar (optional)
Course Ground Sea salt
Fresh ground black pepper

1. Preheat the oven to 375°. Grease a sheet pan with oil.
2. Cut the squash in half and remove the seeds. Place the squash on the sheet pan
    cut side down. Place the pan in the heated oven and roast the squash for 45-50
    minutes or until tender.
3. Allow the squash to cool for 5-10 minutes, then flip them over and dress them
    with pats of butter, salt, pepper and balsamic vinegar or use them for chili bowls
    or to make a squash puree. ℘

Suggested Pairings:
*Classic Roast
Chicken (pg 29),
BEST Salad (pg 54),
Kale Chop Salad
(pg 84), Apple
Cheddar Salad
with Maple
Vinaigrette (pg 100),
Chocolate Honey
Nut Chippers
(pg 110), Zucchini
Fudge Brownies
(pg 122), Fruit
Crisp (pg 123).*

Prep Time:
10 minutes

Cook Time:
2 ½-3 hours, oven;
3 ½ hours, high
heat or 7 hours
low heat, slow
cooker

Yields:
6 servings

Gram's Slow Roasted Country BBQ Ribs with Apple Cheddar Salad and Crispy Tater Chips

The scent of these tasty babies cooking smells so good that you may find neighbors at your door.

Ingredients:

3-4 lbs. country style pork ribs
1 ½-2 tsp. sea salt
1 tsp. ground black pepper
1 tsp. garlic powder
½ tsp. smoked paprika (optional)
1 ½ cups (10 ounces) all natural BBQ sauce (no corn syrup or preservatives)

¼ cup minced onion
½ cup minced fresh parsley, minced
2-3 cloves garlic, chopped
¼ cup water

*Cook's Note: Reserve the pan juices after roasting. The left over rib meat will make delicious **Pulled Pork Sandwiches**. Simply remove the cooked pork from the bone, cut into small pieces and warm with the reserved pan juices.*

1. Preheat the oven 350° and have ready a large casserole dish for roasting.
2. In a small bowl combine the salt, pepper and garlic powder. Rub the spice mixture all over the ribs. Place the ribs in the baking dish or place them in the bottom of a slow cooker. Be sure they fit snuggly.
5. Top the ribs with the BBQ sauce, onions, garlic and parsley. Pour the water around the ribs, cover the dish and place it in the heated oven. Reduce the temperature to 325° and slow roast for 2 ½ -3 hours. They also can be cooked in the slow cooker for 3 ½ hours on high or 7 hours on low. Serve the ribs hot with a spoon of pan juices over top. ℘

Apple Cheddar Salad with Maple Vinaigrette

Ingredients:

Maple Vinaigrette:

⅓ cup raw apple cider vinegar

¼ cup pure maple syrup

¼ cup minced onion or shallot

1 tsp. sea salt

¼ tsp. ground black pepper

¼ cup olive oil

Salad:

8 cups (10 ounces) mixed greens or spinach

2 cups thinly sliced apple

½ cup carrots, cut into match sticks

½ cup organic raisins

½ cup shredded sharp cheddar cheese

¼ cup super-toasty walnuts (pg 15)

1. In a large bowl whisk together the vinegar, maple syrup, onion, salt, pepper and olive oil. Toss in the greens.
2. Gently toss in the apple, carrot, raisins and sharp cheddar cheese. Garnish with walnuts and serve. ⁊

Prep Time:
10 minutes

Yields:
6 servings

Cook's Note: The naturally sweet and tangy vinaigrette will pair well with a variety of greens, fruit and veggie combinations. I like to use it in salads that have roasted beet and squash.

Crispy Tater Chips and Onions

Ingredients:

1 ¼ pounds red or gold potatoes, washed and sliced 1/4 inch thick (4 cups)

1 medium onion, sliced 1/4 inch thick (2 cups)

¾ tsp. sea salt

½ tsp. ground black pepper

2 ½ Tbsp. olive oil

½ cup fresh parsley, minced (optional)

1. Preheat the oven 400°.
2. In a large bowl toss together the potatoes, onion, salt, pepper and olive oil.
3. Spread the potatoes and onion on a baking sheet in a single layer. Place them in the heated oven and bake for 40-50 minutes, until onions are crispy brown.
4. Immediately transfer the potatoes to a large serving bowl, toss with chopped parsley and serve. ⁊

Prep Time:
10 minutes

Bake Time:
40-50 minutes

Marinade time:
6-24 hours

Prep Time:
10 minutes

Cook Time:
45-50 minutes

Yields:
4-6 servings

Sesame Tandoori Chicken with Honey

Mmmm, one of my favorite dishes; succulent, crispy tandoori spice with an accent of honey is oh so nice.

Ingredients:

2-3 lbs. chicken leg quarters

¾ cup plain yogurt

3 cloves garlic

1-2 in. piece ginger, peeled and roughly chopped

2 Tbsp. honey

2 tsp. salt

2 tsp. cumin

1 tsp. paprika

½ tsp. turmeric or curry powder

½ tsp. ground cayenne or black pepper

¾ cup sesame seeds

1 tsp. sea salt

Olive oil or melted ghee

Raw honey for garnish

1. Plan to marinate the chicken 6-24 hours before cooking. To prepare the marinade, use a food processor or blender and puree together the yogurt, garlic, ginger, honey, salt, cumin, paprika, curry powder and pepper. Wash the chicken, place it in a container and coat with the marinade. Store in the fridge for 6-24 hours. Allow the marinating chicken to rest at room temperature 45 minutes prior to baking.

2. Preheat the oven 400°. Place the sesame seeds in a shallow bowl. Have ready a broiler pan or sheet pan, lightly greased with olive oil.

3. Remove the chicken from the marinade and then dip the top side of each piece of chicken in the seeds and place, seed side up, on the broiler pan. Drizzle the chicken with olive oil or melted ghee and place it in the oven. Reduce the temperature to 375° and bake for 50-60 minutes or until the cooked throught. Serve the chicken hot, drizzled with raw honey and your favorite hot sauce. ᘓ

Suggested Pairings:
Fruit Smoothies (pg 56), Kale Chips (pg 59), Red Rebel Soup (pg 71), Coconut Rice Salad with Cilantro-Lime Vinaigrette (pg 80), Harvest Bisque (pg 72), Roasted Brussels Sprouts (pg 85), Yummy Yam Fries (pg 94), Zucchini Fudge Brownies (pg 122)

Prep Time:
25 minutes

Cook Time:
45 minutes

Yields:
6 servings

Cauliflower Puttenesca

The flavors of this dish are a combination of my favorite Italian flavors. It's a tasty and easy way to transform a cauliflower or eggplant into a delicious dish for the whole family.

Ingredients:

1 head cauliflower cut into small pieces (about 6 cups)

3 Tbsp. olive oil or ghee

1 medium onion, peeled and diced

½ tsp. sea salt

1 ½ tsp. dry oregano

½ tsp. ground black pepper

1 ½ Tbsp. (4-5 cloves) fresh garlic, minced

1 28-ounce can diced tomatoes

⅔ cup sliced Kalamata olives

1-2 Tbsp. capers

2-3 Tbsp. lemon juice

¾ cup minced fresh parsley

¼ tsp. crushed red pepper (optional)

Grated sharp Italian cheese or feta cheese for garnish (optional)

1. Heat a large saute pan over med-high heat, add the oil and onions and cook for 2-3 minutes.
2. Reduce the heat to medium and add the cauliflower or eggplant and sauté for 3-5 minutes.
3. Next, add the garlic, pepper and oregano and cook for an additional 2-3 minutes.
4. Add the tomatoes to the pan, bring to a simmer, reduce heat to low, cover and cook for 45 minutes.
5. Stir in the olives, capers, lemon juice, parsley and red pepper and cook for 2-3 minutes longer. Serve with your favorite sides such as garlic toast, Everyday Italian Salad (pg 89) and prepared simple proteins too such as fried eggs (pg 36) or Chicken Tenders (pg 41). 🙰

Cook's Note: For Eggplant Puttenesca substitute one large eggplant. Dice the eggplant 45 minutes before cooking. place it in a colander over a large bowl and toss with sea salt to release excess moisture. Wipe the excess liquid off with a paper towel prior to cooking. Serve topped with cheese and a side of garlic toast.

Prep Time:
45 minutes

Marinade Time:
8-24 hours

Cook Time:
3 ½ hours

Yields:
12-16 servings

Meatballs and Marinara with Kale Pesto Rice

Slow cooked homemade sauce with meatballs is a tradition in my mostly Italian family. Growing up, my mother prepared it almost every week. The day-long preparation was quite consuming but the result was always delicious. With this modified recipe I enjoy treating my family to the same yummy feast without all the fuss.

Ingredients:

Meatballs:

2 lbs. ground pork

1 lb. ground beef

¾ cup grated sharp Italian cheese

1 small onion, peeled

¾ cup fresh parsley

2-3 cloves garlic, peeled

2 large eggs

2 Tbsp. plain yogurt or sour cream

2 Tbsp. dry red wine

1 ½ tsp. sea salt

¾ tsp. ground black pepper

1 tsp. dried oregano

½ tsp. red chili flakes (optional)

Marinara Sauce:

2-3 Tbsp. olive oil

2 cloves garlic minced

2 28-ounce cans organic crushed tomatoes

2 24-ounce jars prepared organic tomato sauce

¾ cup fresh parsley, minced

Salt and pepper to taste

Cook's Note: These meatballs are so tasty; we even eat them for breakfast with a fried egg and garlic toast or roasted spaghetti squash (pg 99).

1. For optimum flavor, prepare the meatball mixture a day before cooking. Place the ground pork, beef and cheese in a large mixing bowl. (I use my stand mixer for this.) Then in a food processor or blender puree together the onion, parsley, garlic, eggs, yogurt, wine, salt, pepper and oregano. Pour the onion mixture over

the meat and mix well to combine. Cover and store in the fridge for up to 24 hours.

2. Preheat the oven 375 degrees. Line a baking sheet with parchment paper. Roll the meat into 2-3 inch balls and place on the baking sheet. Bake the meatballs in the heated oven for 20-25 minutes.

3. Meanwhile, start the sauce by sautéing the olive oil and garlic in a large sauce pan over low heat. Add the crushed tomatoes, tomato sauce and prepared meatballs. Bring the mixture to a simmer and cook over low heat for 2-3 hours. Stir in the parsley and add salt and pepper to taste. Serve over *Kale Pesto Rice* (pg 105), prepared pasta or roasted spaghetti squash with butter. ℘

Prep Time:
15 minutes

Soak Time:
8-20 hours

Cook Time:
45-50 minutes

Yields:
10-12 servings

Kale Pesto Rice

This green goodness can be used in so many ways. Keep it on hand for all your pesto needs.

Ingredients:

2 cups brown rice
4 cups water
1 ¼ tsp. sea salt, divided
6 cups roughly chopped fresh kale
1 cup fresh basil leaves or parsley
2-3 cloves garlic
2 Tbsp. fresh lemon juice
2 tsp. raw honey

¼ tsp. ground black pepper
⅔ cup grated sharp Italian cheese
½ cup olive oil
¼ cup super-toasty walnuts, pecans
** or additional cheese**
1 cup thawed peas (optional)

1. To enhance the rice, soak it for 8-12 hours before cooking (see pg 19).

2. Meanwhile, prepare the pesto. In a food processor, combine the kale, basil, garlic, lemon juice, honey, ¼ tsp. sea salt, pepper, cheese, olive oil and nuts.

3. When ready to cook, rinse and drain the rice and place it in a medium pan with 4 cups water and 1 tsp sea salt. Bring it to a simmer over medium heat, then reduce the heat to low, cover with a lid, and continue cooking for 45 minutes.

4. Immediately stir in the prepared pesto and peas into the hot cooked rice and serve, topped with *Meatballs and Marinara* (pg 104) or with fresh tomatoes, basil and premium balsamic vinegar, *Chicken Tenders* (pg 41) or *Broiled White Fish* (pg 38). ℘

Cook's Note: The kale pesto can be prepared up to 3 days in advance and stored in the fridge. The pesto also freezes well and can be stored for up to 4 months. It tastes wonderful tossed with cooked organic pasta or spread on pizza dough too.

Prep Time:
20 minutes

Cook Time:
10 minutes

Yields:
6-8 servings

Pecan Crusted Pork Tenderloin with Pear Cream and Maple Balsamic Root Salad

Bring bliss to your loved ones lips wit this fabulous dish! A wonderful meal for the Holiday season.

Ingredients:

Pecan Pork Tenderloin:

2 lb. pork tenderloin, sliced ¾ inch thick
¾ cup super-toasty or toasted pecans (see pgs.)
2 tsp. lemon zest
¼ cup fresh parsley
¾ tsp. coriander
½ tsp. cardamom
1 ½ tsp. sea salt
½ tsp. pepper
2 Tbsp. butter
1 Tbsp. olive oil

Sauce:

2 Tbsp. butter or ghee
⅓ cup shallots or onion, minced
¼ tsp. sea salt
4 Bosc pears, sliced, plus additional for garnish
2-3 Tbsp. lemon juice
¼ cup white wine
¼ cup brandy
⅔ cup apple juice
3 Tbsp. milk
½ cup sour cream
¼ cup fresh parsley, minced

Cook's Note:
For entertaining ease, have all ingredients ready prior to cooking. The pecan coating can be prepared 2 days ahead of time and stored in the fridge until ready to cook. Also, the sliced pork can be browned on the edges and set aside for up to an hour, then cooked through in the sauce just before serving.

1. Place the pecans, zest, parsley and spices in a food processor. Pulse until the mixture is finely ground. Place the mixture in a shallow dish and coat each slice of pork; set them on a platter.
2. Heat a large skillet over med-high heat, melt the butter and oil. When just beginning to sizzle, add the pork slices to the pan. Cook for 1-2 minutes on each

side, reduce the heat if they are browning too fast. Quickly remove them from the pan, cover with foil and set aside. Reserve the juices in the pan to prepare the sauce.

3. Combine the sliced pears and lemon juice in a small bowl and set it aside.
4. For the sauce reheat the large skillet over medium heat. Add the 2 Tbsp. butter and the shallot to the pan and sauté for 2 minutes, then add the sliced pears and cook for another 2 minutes. Add the wine, simmer for 1 minute, then add the brandy and simmer for another minute. Next, whisk in the milk, sour cream and parsley. Place the sliced pork back into the pan; simmer until the meat is cooked through. Garnish with fresh pear and minced parsley and serve. ℰℴ

Prep Time:
15 minutes

Cook Time:
40 minutes

Yields:
4 servings

Maple Balsamic Root Salad
Warm autumn sweetness in every bite.

Ingredients:

1 ½ cup beets, peeled and quartered (2-3)

1 ½ cup yam or sweet potato, peeled and sliced in wedges (1 medium)

1 cup sliced carrot

¾ cup sliced onion or shallot

1 tsp. dried thyme or 1 Tbsp. fresh

1 tsp. dried rosemary or 1 Tbsp. fresh

1 tsp. fennel seed

½ tsp. sea salt

2-3 Tbsp. pure maple syrup

3 Tbsp. water

¼ cup balsamic vinegar

5 cups chopped tender chard, beet greens or spinach

3 Tbsp. olive oil or melted ghee

¼ cup super-toasty or toasted walnuts (pg 15) (optional)

¼ cup crumbled goat cheese or shaved Romano cheese (optional)

Shaved fresh fennel (optional)

Suggested Pairings:
Steaks or Lamb Chops (pg 43), Chicken and Veggie Soup (pg 31), Red Rebel soup (pg 71), Black Berry Cheese Squares (pg 124)

1. Preheat the oven 375°. Grease a large (3 qt.) casserole dish with olive oil or ghee.
2. In a large bowl, toss together the beets, yam, carrots, onion, thyme, rosemary, fennel seed, salt and maple syrup. Add the water to the pan, cover and bake for 30 minutes. Uncover and bake for an additional 20 minutes. Remove from the oven and stir in the balsamic vinegar. Keep the dish covered until ready to toss with the greens.
3. In a large bowl, toss together the roasted veggies with their juices, the greens, oil and nuts. Garnish with the goat cheese and fresh fennel and serve. ℰℴ

Vanessa's Kitchen - Pure Food Joy!

Pure Goodies: Cookies, Cakes and other Unrefined Bakes

These guilt-free delights will never spoil an appetite. They are wholesome treats with a heavenly taste. The recipes range from whole grain, to gluten free, sugar free and vegan too. *Pure Food Essentials* (pg 5) will help keep proper ingredients on hand so that preparation is a breeze. They are perfect sweets for a packed lunch, quick snack and many special occasions throughout the year. Enjoy!༝

Prep Time:
15 minutes

Bake Time:
8 minutes

Yields:
24 cookies

Chocolate Honey Nut Chippers

These oooey, gooey, chocolate peanut butter bites are irresistible, secretly nutritious and gluten free. Make one batch or two; super easy to do. Chill them so they are ready for breakfast and lunch.

*Cook's Note:
If using a fresh ground peanut butter with no other additives use 4 Tbsp. butter and ¼ tsp. sea salt.*

Ingredients:

½ cup natural crunchy peanut butter

⅓ cup honey

3 Tbsp. butter, softened

1 large egg

½ tsp. pure vanilla extract

4 ½ Tbsp. unsweetened cocoa powder

3 ½ Tbsp. tapioca flour (gluten free) or all-purpose flour

½ tsp. baking soda

¼ tsp. baking powder

⅛ tsp. sea salt

½ cup chocolate chips

1. Have all ingredients ready at room temperature. Preheat the oven 350° and lightly grease 2 baking sheets.
2. In a large bowl, cream the peanut butter, honey and butter. Mix in the egg and vanilla.
3. In a small bowl, combine the cocoa powder, arrowroot, baking soda and salt. Gradually mix the cocoa mixture into the peanut butter mixture, then fold in the chips.
4. Place 1 tsp. of the batter in rows, 2 inches apart. Place the cookies in the oven and bake for 8-10, minutes. Cool cookies completely and store in a tin in the cupboard for up 5 days or store them in the fridge for up to 2 weeks. ℘

Fudgy Cream Frosting

Creamy and smooth, a truffle-like frosting that is sure to delight. This is an elegant topping for chocolatey cakes, brownies or bars.

Ingredients:

**10 ounces (1 ½ cup) semisweet
  chocolate pieces**
2 Tbsp. strong brewed coffee

4 Tbsp. softened butter, divided
3/4 cup sour cream
2 tsp. pure vanilla extract

1. Using a pan or double boiler, melt together the chocolate, coffee and 1 Tbsp. butter.
2. Remove the chocolate from the heat and stir in the remaining butter, sour cream and vanilla. Spread the frosting immediately on the cake or bars and store it in the fridge until serving. ℘

*Cook's Note:
These are my go to
frostings for so
many cakes and
bakes. The frosting
will solidify once
chilled. It will last
in the fridge for
1 week or the freezer
for 2 months.*

Almond Cream Frosting

Creamy, sweet frosting as healthy as can be that is sure to please.

Ingredients:

**8 ounce cream cheese, (room
  temperature)**
**1 cup (2 sticks) butter (room
  temperature)**

**2/3 cup raw honey, the firm type will
  work best**
1 Tbsp. almond extract

1. In medium bowl whip the cream cheese with a spoon. Then add the butter and whip together until smooth. Then stir in the honey and almond extract.
2. Spread the icing over the prepared cake or cakes while it is still soft. Then chill the cakes in the fridge for at least 2 hours before serving. ℘

Prep Time:
15 minutes

Yields:
16 truffles
Gluten Free

Coconut Lime Truffles

A yummy, raw food treat that will help curb the craving for something sweet. Package them up for everyday or enjoy them on a holiday.

Ingredients:

1 ½ cups chopped pitted dates

¾ cup super-toasty or toasted pecans, walnuts or sunflower seeds (see pg 15)

1 ¼ cup toasted flaked coconut, divided (see pg 15)

2 Tbsp. raw honey

1-2 tsp. fresh lime zest

2-3 Tbsp. lime juice (1-2 limes)

½ tsp sea salt

Cook's Note: For a different flavor twist try Lemon Coconut Truffles simply substitute the lime zest and juice for the same amount of lemon zest and juice.

1. Using a food processor combine dates, pecans, ½ cup coconut, honey, lime zest, lime juice and salt in a food processor. Pulse 2-3 times in at first and then puree the mixture until a smooth paste has formed (about 45 seconds).

2. With damp hands roll the mixture into 1 inch size balls. Then roll them in the toasty coconut, store in the fridge or freezer until serving. ℘

Prep Time:
20 minutes

Bake Time:
60 minutes total

Yields:
1 loaf

Baked Banana Date and Nut Bread

A wholesome, moist, banana-ee bread.

Ingredients:

4 very ripe bananas

8 Tbsp. butter or coconut oil

⅔ cup natural brown sugar (pg 9)

2 large eggs

1 tsp. pure vanilla extract

½ cup sour cream or plain whole milk
   yogurt

1 ⅔ cup whole wheat flour or whole
   grain spelt flour

1 tsp. baking powder

½ tsp. baking soda

¼ tsp. sea salt

1 tsp. ground cinnamon

½ tsp. ground nutmeg

½ cup super-toasty or plain walnuts,
   chopped (pg 15) (optional)

½ cup chopped pitted dates

Cook's Note:
Baking the
bananas enhances
the flavor. This is
an optional step.
I like to wrap
individual slices of
this bread and freeze
so it is ready for an
easy grab-and-go
snack or breakfast.

1. Preheat the oven 400°. Place the bananas, with the peel on, in a small baking dish. Bake for 15 minutes until the skin has turned black and the inside is soft. Remove them from the oven and cool.

2. Have all the ingredients ready at room temperature. Preheat the oven 350°, grease and flour 1 standard-size loaf pan.

3. Remove the peel from the bananas and place them in a food processor along with the butter, brown sugar, eggs, vanilla and sour cream; puree the mixture until smooth.

4. In a small bowl combine the flour, baking powder, baking soda, salt, cinnamon and nutmeg. Gradually add the flour mixture to the banana mixture in the food processor; process until smooth. Then add in the walnuts and dates and pulse 8 times.

5. Pour the batter into the prepared pan and bake for 45-50 minutes.

Prep Time:
10 minutes

Bake Time:
25-35 minutes

Yields:
Two 9-inch cakes
or 24 cupcakes

Carrot Cakes with Cinnamon Cream Frosting

This super moist classic cake with a guilt-free wholesome twist is perfect for your next holiday brunch or birthday gathering.

Ingredients:

6 Tbsp. butter or coconut oil, melted

1 cup natural brown sugar (pg 9)

1 20-ounce can crushed pineapple with juice

Juice and zest of 1 large orange

4 large eggs

1 tsp. pure vanilla extract

2 Tbsp. spiced rum (optional)

2 Tbsp. plain yogurt or sour cream

2 cups whole grain spelt flour or whole wheat flour

2 tsp. baking powder

2 tsp. baking soda

½ tsp. sea salt

1 ½ tsp. ground cinnamon

½ tsp. ground ginger

¼ tsp. ground nutmeg

2 cups carrots, shredded

½ cup raisins

½ cup super-toasty walnuts (pg 15), chopped (optional)

1 recipe *Cinnamon Cream Frosting*

Cook's Note:
This cake recipe can be baked into any size you like. Look at step #5 for the baking variations.

1. Preheat the oven 350°, grease, flour and/or line your pan of choice

2. In a large mixing bowl combine the butter, natural brown sugar, orange juice and zest, rum, pineapple, eggs, vanilla and yogurt. Beat on medium speed for 1 minute until well combined.

3. In another large bowl mix together the flour, baking powder, soda, salt, cinnamon, ginger and nutmeg. Then stir in the carrots, raisins, walnuts.

4. Gradually add the flour mixture into the pineapple mixture. Beat on medium

---

speed for one minute until well combined. Let the batter rest for 1-4 hours before baking for optimum texture and flavor.

5. Divide the batter into the prepared pan or pans and place in the warm oven and bake. For a 9x13 in. pan and 9 in. cake pans bake for 30-35 minutes, for cupcakes or muffins bake for 25-30 minutes or until a toothpick comes out clean. Remove the cakes from the oven cool completely, frost and chill. ℘

Cinnamon Cream Frosting

Ingredients:

8 ounce cream cheese, (room
temperature)

1 cup (2 sticks) butter, (room
temperature)

⅔ cup raw honey, the firm type will
work best

2 tsp. pure vanilla extract

½ tsp. ground cinnamon

1. In medium bowl cream the cream cheese. Then add the softened butter, honey, vanilla and cinnamon; cream together until smooth.

2. Spread the icing over the prepared cake or cakes while it is still soft. Dust the tops with cinnamon then chill the cakes in the fridge for at least 2 hours before serving. ℘

Prep Time:
5 minutes

Yields:
2 ½ cups
frosting

Cook's Note:
The frosting will
solidify once chilled.
Also a basic **Honey**
Cream Frosting
can be prepared
by omitting the
cinnamon and
Almond Cream
Frosting *can be*
made as well ,
see pg 111.

Prep Time:
20 minutes

Cook Time:
35-40 minutes

Yields:
Two 9 inch
cake layers

Suggested Pairings:
Chicken Tenders
(pg 41), Broiled
White Fish (pg 38),
Asparagus Bisque
(pg 69), Lemon
Veggie Quinoa Salad
(pg 82), Kale Pesto
Rice (pg 105).

Strawberry Lemon Almond Cream Cake

This delightful cake is the perfect showcase for summer's bounty of berries. This tall treat is a great way to celebrate birthdays that fall during those beautiful balmy days.

Ingredients:

Cake:

1 ¼ cup super-toasty or toasted
  almonds (see pg 15)

¾ cup pure cane sugar, divided

8 ounces cream cheese, (room
  temperature)

8 large eggs, separated

1 tsp. almond extract

2 tsp lemon zest

⅓ cup lemon juice (1-2 large lemons)

⅛ tsp. sea salt

Honey Almond Whip:

2 cups heavy cream, chilled

½ cup raw honey

1 ½ Tbsp. pure almond extract

Strawberry Topping:

2 pounds fresh strawberries, cleaned
  and stems trimmed

2 Tbsp. raw honey, divided

2 Tbsp. cognac blended orange
  liquor (see pg 10), divided

1. Have all cake ingredients ready at room temperature. Preheat the oven 350°. Grease two 9 inch cake pans, line them with parchment paper and grease again (this will help the cakes remove easily).

2. Using a food processor combine the almonds and ¼ cup sugar process them into a fine crumb. Then add in the cream cheese, egg yolks and almond extract, process for 1 minute until a paste has formed. Then add in the lemon zest, lemon

juice and salt and process for another minute. Transfer the mixture to a large mixing bowl.

3. In another large mixing bowl using an electric mixer beat the egg whites on high speed. Gradually add in the remaining ½ cup sugar beat on high speed for 2-3 minutes until stiff peaks form. Stir ⅓ of the beaten egg whites into the almond mixture. Then gently fold in the remaining egg whites.

4. Pour the batter into the prepared pans (the batter will fill most of the pans), place in the center of the oven and bake 33-40 minutes or until set. Cool the cakes completely. Then line two large dinner plates with parchment or wax paper. Invert the cakes onto each plate and place them in the fridge until ready to assemble the whole cake.

5. Meanwhile prepare the berries. Slice 1 ½ cups of the berries for the center of the cake. Place the sliced berries in a medium bowl with 1 Tbsp. of honey and 1 Tbsp. orange liquor, toss until coated. Reserve the remaining whole strawberries for the top of the cake.

6. Prepare the *Honey Almond Whip*. Using a large mixing bowl beat the heavy cream on high speed for 1 minute. Once it begins to thicken add in the honey and then continue to beat on high speed for 2-3 minutes or until stiff peaks form. Then add in the almond extract and beat for 30 more seconds.

7. To assemble the cake place one of the layers on the serving plate, top the sliced berries and honey mixture and ⅓ of the *Honey Almond Whip*. Add the second cake layer, dollop on the remaining whip cream and then arrange the whole berries on top. Whisk together the remaining honey and orange liquor and drizzle over the berries for a shiny glaze. Chill the cake until serving time.

Cook's Note:
The cake layers can be prepared a day or two ahead of time and stored in the fridge or freezer until ready to assemble. For the best whip cream, chill the beaters and bowl before whipping.

Prep time:
25 minutes

Cook time:
50-60 minutes

Yields:
8-10 servings

Chocolate Raspberry Torte

Mi Amore, Chocolate! A true elixir of love. Set your hearts a buzz with this sensual delight. It pairs well with a smooth glass of wine as your evening winds down or with an AM cup of jo while you reminisce about the night before.

Ingredients:

Cocoa Nut Crust: (gluten free)
⅔ cup super-toasty or toasted almonds (see pg 15)
⅔ cup toasted coconut (see pg 15)
⅓ cup chopped pitted dates
⅓ cup semi-sweet chocolate chips
1 Tbsp. unsweetened cocoa powder
¼ tsp. sea salt
1 ½ Tbsp. raw honey or pure cane sugar
1 ½ tsp. pure vanilla or almond extract

Chocolate Raspberry Mousse:
2 Tbsp. butter or coconut oil
⅔ cup semi-sweet chocolate chips
2 Tbsp. brewed espresso or strong coffee
⅓ cup whole fruit raspberry preserves
¼ cup pure cane sugar
½ cup cocoa powder
2 tsp. vanilla

2 large eggs, separated
⅔ cup chilled heavy cream
¼ tsp. sea salt

Chocolate Ganache Glaze:
¼ cup heavy cream
⅓ cup semisweet chocolate chips
2 Tbsp. brewed espresso or strong coffee
1 ½ tsp. vanilla extract

Toppings:
1 pint fresh organic raspberries
1 recipe *Honey Almond Whip* (pg 126)

*Cook's Note: This torte can be prepared with a **Chocolate Cookie Crust**. Simply combine 2 ½ cups chocolate wafer cookies in a food processor with 2 Tbsp. pure cane sugar and 3 Tbsp. melted butter. I suggest freezing this cake because it slices easier when frozen. It can be kept in the fridge too.*

1. Grease 1 8 or 9 inch spring form pan.
2. To prepare the crust, combine the almonds, coconut, dates, chocolate chips, cocoa powder and salt in a food processor; grind to a fine crumb. Then add the honey; process until well combined. Press the crumb mixture into the greased spring form pan. Chill the crust while the *Chocolate Raspberry Mousse* is prepared.
3. Preheat the oven to 325° and position the rack in the center of the oven.
4. To prepare the *Chocolate Raspberry Mousse*, place the butter and chocolate chips and hot espresso in a medium sauce pan. Melt the mixture over low heat, stirring often, until it is smooth; remove from heat.
5. Meanwhile, in a large bowl whisk together the egg yolks, raspberry preserves, sugar, and vanilla. Gradually whisk in the cocoa powder. Then whisk in the melted chocolate mixture until well combined.
6. Using an electric mixer, beat the egg whites and salt on high speed for 1-2 minutes or until firm peaks have formed. Gently fold the beaten whites into the chocolate mixture.
7. Next, using an electric mixer, beat the cream over high speed until stiff peaks have formed. Gently fold the whipped cream into the chocolate mixture.
8. Pour the batter into the prepared pan and bake for 50 minutes. Turn the oven off and let the cake set in the warm oven for an additional 10 minutes.
9. Cool the cake completely, and chill.
10. Prepare the *Chocolate Ganache Glaze*. Place the chocolate chips in a medium bowl. Heat the cream over medium heat until just boiling, then pour the hot cream over the chocolate; let it set for 5 minutes, then whisk until smooth. Whisk in the extract, then pour the chocolate ganache over the chilled cake. Store the torte in the freezer. Remove the cake from the freezer about 30-40 minutes before serving. Top it with fresh raspberries and serve with *Honey Whip* (pg 126).

Cook's Note:
Grilled Steak (pg 38), Rosemary Roasted Potatoes (pg 97), Kale Chop Salad (pg 84), Eggplant Puttenesca (pg 103), Everyday Italian Salad (pg 89), Meatballs and Marinara with Kale Pesto Rice (pg 104).

Prep Time:
40 minutes

Bake Time:
60 minutes

Yields:
8-10 servings
Gluten Free

Apricot Ricotta Cheese Cake with Fruit

This light and creamy dessert beautifully displays the fruits of the season. It has also become a family favorite at our annual 4th of July gathering, using blue berries and strawberries in patriotic shapes.

Ingredients:

Macaroon Crust:
⅔ cup super-toasty almonds or toasted almonds (see pg 15)
⅔ cup chopped pitted dates
⅔ cup toasted coconut flakes (see pg 15)
1 tsp. ground cinnamon
⅛ tsp. sea salt
1 Tbsp. raw honey or pure cane sugar
2 tsp. almond extract

Apricot Ricotta Filling:
(have all ingredients at room temperature)
1 8-ounce package cream cheese, softened
1 cup whole milk ricotta cheese, strained
¾ cup whole fruit apricot preserves
2 large eggs
1 tsp. almond or vanilla extract

Fruit Topping:
2 pounds fresh seasonal fruit (strawberries, blue berries, sliced kiwi, nectarines, peaches, apples and mandarin oranges)
⅓ cup whole fruit apricot preserves
2 Tbsp. raw honey
1 tsp. almond extract (optional)

Cook's Note: A Graham Cracker crust can be substituted for the Macaroon Crust. Combine 1½ cups graham crackers in a food processor with 3 Tbsp. pure cane sugar and 4 Tbsp. melted butter

1. Preheat the oven 350°. Grease an 8" spring form pan with butter or coconut oil.
2. To make the crust, combine the almonds, dates and coconut in a food processor; puree into a fine crumble. Add the cinnamon, salt, honey and almond extract and puree again. Press the mixture into the prepared pan and chill in the fridge while you prepare the filling.
3. To prepare the filling, combine the cream cheese, ricotta cheese, apricot preserves, eggs and extract in a food processor or blender. Puree for 1-2 minutes until smooth and then pour into the prepared crust. Place the cake on a baking sheet in the center of the oven. Bake for 45 minutes, until just set. Turn off the oven and allow for the cake to rest in the oven for 10 minutes longer. Then remove it from the oven and cool. Store the cake in the refrigerator or freezer until you're ready to add the fruit topping.
4. On the day of serving arrange the prepared fruit over the top of the chilled cake. In a small sauce pan, warm the apricot preserves and honey. Stir in the almond extract, then brush the glaze over the fruit. Chill for at least 1 hour prior to serving. When ready to serve, run a knife around the outer rim of the crust and remove the outer rim of the spring pan; slice and serve.

Cook's Note:
This cake can be baked ahead of time and stored in the fridge (2 days) or freezer (2 months) until a special occasion arises.

Prep Time:
15 minutes

Bake Time:
20-25 minutes

Yields:
12 brownies

Zucchini Fudge Brownies

Oooey, gooey and gluten free! There are so many fun way to enjoy these, check out the Cook's Note.

Ingredients:

6 Tbsp. coconut oil or butter

1 cup semisweet chocolate chips, divided

2 Tbsp. strong brewed coffee or milk

1 tsp. pure vanilla extract

1 cup packed shredded zucchini

½ cup pure cane sugar or coconut sugar

2 large eggs + 2 yolks

½ cup tapioca flour or arrowroot powder (gluten free) or all-purpose flour

⅓ cup unsweetened cocoa powder

½ tsp. baking powder

½ tsp. baking soda

½ tsp. sea salt

1. Preheat the oven 350°. Have ready a greased 13x9 inch baking dish. Melt the coconut oil over low heat on the stove, then gradually add ⅔ cup of the chocolate chips and melt. Stir in the coffee and vanilla.

2. In a large bowl, combine the zucchini, sugar and eggs.

3. In a small bowl, combine together the flour, cocoa powder, baking powder, baking soda and salt.

4. Add the cocoa powder mixture to the zucchini mixture. Mix until well combined, then stir in the melted chocolate and fold in the remaining ⅓ cup chocolate chips. Pour the batter into the prepared pan.

5. Bake for 20-25 minutes or until set. Store the brownies in the fridge for up to 1 week or in the freezer for up to 6 weeks. ℘

*Cook's Note:
I love to whip up a batch of these delicious brownies to enjoy as a base for ice cream sundaes, Zucchini Fudge Brownies ala Mode. I also wrap and freeze them for an easy grab-and-go sweet bite for Dad's morning off-to-work. For a rich and decadent dessert, I like to top them with Fudgy Cream Frosting (pg 111) and piped Almond Cream Frosting (pg 111).*

Prep Time:
20 minutes

Rest Time:
3-24 hours

Bake Time:
35 minutes

Yields:
6-8 servings

Fruit Crisp

An easy, sweet dish that tastes as good as pie. A wonderful way to enjoy the abundant fruits of the season.

Ingredients:

⅔ **cup rolled oats**

⅔ **cup +1 Tbsp. all-purpose flour**

½ **cup +2 Tbsp. turbinado, pure cane sugar or coconut sugar**

½ **cup toasted walnuts or pecans**

2 **tsp. ground cinnamon, divided**

¼ **tsp. sea salt**

¼ **tsp. freshly grated nutmeg**

3 **Tbsp. plain yogurt or sour cream**

6 **Tbsp. butter, chilled**

6 **cups (2 pounds) seasonal fruits; sliced apples, pears, peaches, cherries and/or berries of choice**

1 ½ **Tbsp. brandy or 1 tsp. pure vanilla extract**

Suggested Pairings:
Classic Chili with Winter Squash Cups (pg 98), Pan Fried Pork Chops with Apple Glaze (pg 45), Frozen Maple Whip (pg 126), Frozen vanilla yogurt or ice cream

1. In a medium bowl, combine together the oats, flour, sugar, walnuts, 1 tsp. cinnamon, nutmeg and yogurt. Allow to rest at room temperature for 3-24 hours to soften the oats.

2. Preheat the oven 375°. Have ready a greased 7x11 inch casserole dish or pie plate. Cut the butter into small cubes and, using a pastry cutter, gently work the butter into the oat mixture until it is a crumby texture.

3. In another medium bowl, toss together the apples, lemon juice and remaining 1 tsp. of cinnamon. Spread the apples on the bottom of the dish, then top with the oat mixture. Place the pan in the heated oven and bake for 35 minutes. Cool for 5 minutes and then serve warm with your favorite frozen toppings. ❧

Black Berry Cheese Squares
Jewels of nature perfectly presented!

Prep Time:
20 minutes

Bake Time:
20-25 minutes

Chill Time:
8-24 hours

Yields:
20 squares

Ingredients:

Walnut Crumb Crust:
¾ cup super-toasty or toasted
  walnuts (see pg 15)
½ cup + 1 Tbsp. whole grain spelt flour
  or all-purpose flour
3 Tbsp. pure cane sugar (pg 9)
1 ½ tsp. ground cinnamon
¼ tsp. salt
2 Tbsp. chilled butter, cut into cubes

Goat Cheese Filling:
8 ounces goat cheese
3 Tbsp. butter
⅓ cup honey or pure cane sugar
2 large eggs
1 tsp. pure vanilla extract

Black Berry Topping:
1 pint fresh organic black berries
½ cup whole fruit blackberry
  preserves
1 Tbsp. raw honey
1 Tbsp. water

Cook's Note:
*8 ounces cream
cheese can be
substituted for the
goat cheese and
butter. If this is
done, reduce the
honey to ¼ cup.*

1. Have all filling ingredients ready at room temperature. Preheat the oven 350°. Grease and flour a 2 qt. baking dish, 11x7 inch or 9x9 inch pan.
2. For the crust, place the walnuts in a food processor and grind until fine. Then add the flour, sugar, cinnamon and salt; process until combined. Add in the butter and pulse the mixture together 8-10 times until well combined. Press the crumb mixture into the prepared pan and bake for 8 minutes.
3. Meanwhile, prepare the filling. Using a food processor or blender, combine the goat cheese, butter, honey, eggs and vanilla; puree until smooth.
4. Pour the filling over the crust. Place in the heated oven and bake for 20-25 minutes, until set. Allow to cool completely and then add the blackberry topping.
5. For the topping, arrange the blackberries in rows about ½ inch apart. In a small pan, warm together the preserves, honey and water; stir until smooth. Drizzle or brush the preserves over the top of the berries. Chill the bars for 2-12 hours before cutting. ∾

Apple Butternut Muffins

These whole grain autumn bites are filled with moist, warm flavors.

Prep Time:
25 minutes

Bake Time:
20-25 minutes

Yields:
15-18 muffins

Ingredients:

1 small butternut squash	1 ½ cups + 2 Tbsp. whole grain flour
2 cups peeled, sliced apples (or substitute ¾ cup apple sauce)	½ cup all-purpose flour
9 Tbsp. softened butter, divided	½ tsp. baking powder
2 lg. eggs (room temperature)	½ tsp. baking soda
½ cup+2 Tbsp. natural brown sugar (pg 9)	¼ tsp. sea salt
½ cup pure cane sugar	1 ½ tsp. ground cinnamon, divided
1 tsp. pure vanilla extract	¼ tsp ground nutmeg
	¼ cup ground super-toasty or toasted walnuts (pg 15)

Cook's Note:
These can be transformed into Apple Pumpkin Muffins by simply substituting one 14 ounce can of pumpkin puree for the butternut squash. Wrap and freeze them for an easy snack on the go.

1. First roast the butternut squash and apples. Preheat the oven 375°. Cut the butternut squash and remove the seeds using a large spoon. Place the squash, cut side down, on a greased pan. Place the sliced apples in a small baking dish and cover with foil. Roast both for 45-60 minutes until tender. Allow to cool.

2. Prepare the streusel topping by combining the walnuts, 2 Tbsp. brown sugar, ½ tsp. ground cinnamon and 1 Tbs. butter in a small bowl. Mix until well combined and set aside.

3. Next, measure 1 ¾ cup of the roasted butternut squash. Place it in a food processer along with the roasted apples. Puree until smooth.

4. Place the remaining 8 Tbs. of the butter in the food processor along with the eggs, sugars and vanilla. Puree until smooth.

5. In a medium bowl, combine the flours, baking powder, baking soda, salt, cinnamon, ginger, nutmeg and cloves. Add the flour mixture gradually to the food processor and puree 2-3 minutes until very smooth.

6. Have ready a lined muffin tin. Fill the muffin cups ¾ full and sprinkle with the prepared topping. Bake in a 350° oven until set, 20-25 minutes. Cool and serve.

Preparation Time:
30 minutes

Bake Time:
45-50 minutes

Yields:
One 9-10 inch pie

Pecan Pumpkin Pie with Maple Whip

Two pies in one; a sure crowd pleaser for your Holiday feast!

Ingredients:

Ginger Snap Crust:

2 ¼ cups natural ginger snap cookies

½ tsp. ground cinnamon

1 Tbsp. pure cane sugar

2 Tbsp. butter, melted

Filling:

have ingredients ready at room temperature

1 pie pumpkin or 1 14-ounce can of pumpkin

⅔ cup pure cane sugar

⅔ cup heavy cream or coconut milk

1 ½ Tbsp. bourbon

2 tsp. pure vanilla extract

2 large eggs + 1 yolk (reserve the white for the pecan topping)

¼ tsp. sea salt

1 ½ tsp. ground cinnamon

½ tsp. ground nutmeg

¼ tsp. ground ginger

¼ tsp. ground cloves

Pecan Topping:

1 egg white

1 cup whole super-toasty or toasted pecans (see pg 15)

3 Tbsp. pure maple syrup

⅛ tsp. sea salt

Maple Whip:

1 ¼ cup heavy whipping cream, chilled

¼ cup pure maple syrup, chilled

1 tsp. pure vanilla extract

1-2 tsp. bourbon (optional)

¼ tsp. ground cinnamon

1. If using a fresh pie pumpkin, it can be roasted a day or two before preparing the pie. Preheat the oven 375°. Cut the pumpkin in half, scoop out the seeds and place, face down, on a greased baking sheet and bake for 45-60 minutes, until tender. Allow the pumpkin to cool, then scoop out the flesh, drain out any excess water and measure 1 ¾ cup for the pie filling.

Cook's Note:
This pie tastes best
the second day after
baking, a wonderful
prepare-ahead
holiday dessert.

*For a **Pumpkin Pie**,*
omit the maple
praline topping
found in step #5.

2. To prepare the pie. Preheat the oven 350°. Grease a 9 or 10-inch pie plate. Place the rack in the center of the oven.

3. For the crust, combine together the ginger snaps, cinnamon and sugar in the food processor; process into a crumb. Add the melted butter and process again for 30 seconds until the crumbs are moistened. Press the mixture into the pie plate and place in the fridge while you prepare the filling.

4. To prepare the filling, combine the pumpkin, sugar, heavy cream, bourbon, vanilla, eggs, salt and spices in a food processor; puree until smooth and pour into the prepared crust. Place the pie on a baking sheet and bake for 35 minutes.

5. Meanwhile, prepare the *Pecan Topping*. In a medium mixing bowl, whisk together the egg white and salt until frothy. Whisk in the maple syrup and cinnamon; fold the pecans into the egg white mixture until coated. Arrange the coated pecans starting around the outer rim of the pie, and continue to spiral them in towards the center until the pie is covered. Drizzle the syrup and egg white mixture over the top to glaze the pecans. Place the pie back in the oven and bake for an additional 25-30 minutes or until the pie is set. Remove from the oven and cool. Run a small, sharp knife around the rim of the crust to prevent sticking.

6. To Prepare the *Maple Whip*, place the chilled whipped cream in a large mixing bowl with an electric beater; beat it on high speed for 1-2 minutes, until soft peaks form. Stop the mixing and add the maple syrup, vanilla, bourbon and cinnamon; continue to beat on high speed for 1-2 minutes or until stiff peaks form. Store in the fridge or freezer and serve with the prepared pie. ∞

Prep time:
20 minutes

Cook time:
40-60 minutes

Yields:
6-8 servings

Figgy Puddin' with Vanilla Brandy Cream

A dreamy treat that is sure to surprise your loved ones. Enjoy this warm, custard dish during the Holidays for breakfast or dessert. The flavors of this dish are amazing!

Ingredients:

Vanilla Brandy Cream:

1 cup heavy whipping cream, chilled
¼ cup raw honey
1 Tbsp. brandy
1 ½ tsp. pure vanilla extract

Pudding:

¾ cup fig preserves
½ cup milk
2 Tbsp. corn flour or tapioca flour
¾ tsp. baking powder
½ tsp. sea salt
½ tsp fresh grated nutmeg
1 cup heavy cream
2 large eggs + 2 large egg yolks
2 tsp. pure vanilla extract

Fruit:

2-3 persimmons, ripened
4-5 fresh figs, sliced

1. First prepare the *Vanilla Brandy Cream*. With an electric mixer and a large bowl, whip the cream on high speed until stiff peaks begin to form. Stop the mixer and add the honey, brandy and vanilla to the cream and continue to whip the cream on high speed for another 1-2 minutes. Transfer the whipped cream to an air tight container and store in the freezer or fridge until serving.
2. Preheat the oven 350°. Grease a 1 qt. oven safe bowl or 6-8 ramekins.
3. Combine the preserves and milk in a medium sauce pan; bring to a simmer over medium heat. Whisk in the cornmeal, baking powder, salt and nutmeg. Whisk for 2 minutes until thick and bubbly.
4. Meanwhile, in a small bowl, combine the cream, eggs and yolks. Gradually whisk the cream and egg mixture into the pan and continue to cook over medium heat until it begins to bubble.
5. Pour the mixed pudding into the prepared baking dish or dishes. When ready to bake, fill a 13 x 9 inch casserole dish with 1 inch hot water to create a water bath. Place the pudding dish in the water bath and place the whole pan in the oven; bake for 40-45 minutes for ramekins or 50-60 minutes if using a large bowl. The pudding is done when it is quivery and set in the middle.
6. Serve the pudding with fresh persimmon and fig slices, topped with a dollop of prepared *Vanilla Brandy Cream*. ✖

Subject Index

This index is a guide to help you find the best recipe for your situation and diet. Take note that all of the recipes in this book are gluten free with the exception of some of the baked goods. Therefore I have only noted only which snacks and desserts are **gluten free**. ℰↃ

Gluten Free Snacks and Desserts

Lunch Box Bites

Quick Dishes

Vegan Recipes

*Disclaimer-The health and nutrition information provided in this book has not been approved by a certified dietician or nutritionist.

Vanessa's Kitchen - Pure Food Joy!

Ingredient Index

This index will guide you to the perfect recipe for the ingredients that you have on hand and ingredients that are in season and on sale in the market. Using this index to create your weekly meals will help to reduce waste, promote seasonal eating and instill shopping and spending efficiency. 🙠

Apple Cider Vinegar (raw), continued

Black Bean, Corn and Avocado Salad pg 79, Coconut Rice Salad with Cilantro-Lime Vinaigrette pg 80, Kale Chopped Salad pg 84, Everyday Italian Salad pg 89, Apricot-Glazed Chops with Carrots pg 92, Strawberry Spinach Salad with Lemon Poppy seed Vinaigrette pg 93, Pineapple Blueberry Slaw pg 94, Apple Cheddar Salad with Maple Vinaigrette pg 101

Apricot

~ *Dried*

Overnight Oats pg 22, Honey Yogurt pg 24, Homemade Greek Yogurt pg 24

~ *Fresh*

Fruit Smoothies pg 56, Fresh Fruit with Mascarpone Dip pg 61, Apricot Ricotta Cheesecake pg 120, Fruit Crisp pg 123

~ *Jam*

Jam recipe pg 50

Arrowroot Powder

~ *about* pg 8

Irish Stew pg 90, Chocolate Honey Nut Chippers pg 110, Zucchini Fudge Brownies pg 122

Artichokes (marinated)

Warm Cheese and Artichoke Dip pg 64

Arugula

Broiled White Fish pg 38, Skillet Shrimp pg 39, Wild Balsamic Salmon with Berries Goat Cheese and Greens pg 40, Chicken Tenders pg 41, Lemon Veggie Quinoa Salad pg 82

Asiago Cheese

Veggie Beef Soup pg 28, Poached Greens N' Eggs in Broth pg 27, Chicken Vegetable Soup pg 31, Family Frittata pg 49, Breakfast Casserole pg 49, Veggie Minestrone pg 68, Tomato Soup Florentine pg 70, Lemon Veggie Quinoa Salad pg 82, Everyday Italian Salad pg 89, Cauliflower Puttenesca pg 103, Eggplant Puttenesca pg 103, Meatballs and Marinara with Kale Pesto Rice pg 104

Asparagus

Family Frittata pg 49, Breakfast Casserole pg 49, Asparagus Bisque pg 69, Lemon Veggie Quinoa Salad pg 82

Avocado

Egg O's and Avo's pg 35, BEST Salad pg 54, Chili N Grits Breakfast Bake with Pico Di Gallo pg 52, Super Nachos and Tacos pg 66, Curry Chicken Salad pg 60, Black Bean, Corn and Avocado Salad pg 79

Beans, continued

~ *Kidney*

about pg 8

Veggie Minestrone pg 68, Classic Chili pg 98, Vegetarian Chili pg 98

~ *Pinto Beans*

Classic Chili pg 98, Super Nachos and Tacos pg 66, Vegetarian Chili pg 98

~ *Refried Beans*

Super Nachos and Tacos pg 66

Beef

~ *Ground*

Super Nachos and Tacos pg 66, Meatballs and Marinara pg 104, Classic Chili pg 98

~ *Soup Bones*

Roasted Beef Bone Broth pg 27, Veggie Beef Soup pg 28, Poached Greens and Eggs in Broth pg 27

~ *Steak*

Steak and Lamb Chops pg 43

~ *Stew Meat*

Irish Stew and Soda Bread pg 90

Beets

Fruit Smoothies pg 56, Red Rebel Soup pg 71, Kale Chopped Salad pg 84, Maple Balsamic Root Salad pg 107

Bell Pepper

~ *Green*

Pico Di Gallo pg 52, Warm Cheese and Artichoke Dip pg 64, Classic Chili pg 98, Vegetarian Chili pg 98

~ *Orange*

Black Bean, Corn and Avocado Salad pg 79

~ *Red*

Warm Cheese and Artichoke Dip pg 64, Red Rebel Soup pg 71, Asian Sesame Slaw pg 76, Coconut Rice with Cilantro Lime Vinaigrette pg 80, Everyday Italian Salad pg 89, Grilled Mahi Mahi with Pineapple Blueberry Slaw pg 94

Belgium Endive-

Egg Salad and Endive pg 62, Curry Chicken Salad pg 60

Blackberries-

Honey Yogurt pg 24, Homemade Greek Yogurt pg 24, Balsamic Salmon with Berries and Goat Cheese pg 40, Berry and Cheese Crepes with Maple-Spiced Nuts pg 50, Fruit Smoothies pg 56, Fresh Fruit and Mascarpone Dip pg 61, Apricot Ricotta Cheesecake with Fruit pg 120, Black Berry Cheese Squares pg 124, Fruit Crisp pg 123

Blueberries-

Honey Yogurt pg 24, Homemade Greek Yogurt pg 24, Balsamic Salmon with Berries and Goat Cheese pg 40, Berry and Cheese Crepes with Maple-Spiced Nuts pg 50, Fruit Smoothies pg 56, Grilled Mahi Mahi with Pineapple Blueberry Slaw pg 94, Apricot Ricotta Cheese Cake with Fruit pg 120, Fruit Crisp pg 123

Blue Cheese-

BEST Salad pg 54, Super Broccoli Salad pg 77, Kale Chopped Salad pg 84, Everyday Italian Salad pg 89, Grilled Orange Balsamic Chicken with Grapes and Rosemary Roasted Potatoes pg 96

Broccoli-

Warm Cheese and Artichoke Dip pg 64, Broccoli Cheddar Bisque pg 72, Super Broccoli Salad pg 77

Broth

~ *Beef*

Roasted Beef Bone Broth pg 27, Veggie Beef Soup pg 28, Poached Greens and Eggs N' Broth pg 27

~ *Chicken*

Homemade pg 29, Chicken Vegetable Soup pg 31, Asparagus Bisque pg 69, Broccoli Cheddar Bisque pg 72, Tomato Soup Florentine pg 70, Red Rebel Soup pg 71

~ *Veggie*

Asparagus Bisque pg 69, Broccoli Cheddar Bisque pg 72, Red Rebel Soup pg 71

Brussel Sprouts

Roasted Brussels Sprouts pg 85

Buck Wheat

~ *flour*

Berry and Cheese Crepes with Maple Spiced Nuts pg 50, Nut Butter and Jam Crepes pg 50

~ *groats* pg 19

Butternut Squash

Harvest Bisque pg 72, Apple Butternut Muffins pg 125

Cabbage

~ *Green*

Asian Sesame Slaw pg 76

~ *Purple*

Egg Salad and Endive pg 62, Super Broccoli Salad pg 77, Kale Chopped Salad pg 84, Everyday Italian salad pg 89, Pineapple Blueberry Slaw pg 94

Carnival Squash

Winter Squash Cups pg 98

Chicken, continued

~ *legs*
  Grilled Cajun Chicken Drummies pg 42, Sesame Tandoori Chicken with Honey pg 102
~ *tenders*
  Chicken Tenders pg 41, Asian Sesame Slaw pg 76, Lemon Veggie Quinoas Salad pg 82,
  Cilantro-Lime Chicken pg 80, Grilled Orange Balsamic Chicken with Grapes and Rosemary
  Roasted Potatoes pg 96
~ *whole roasted*
  Classic Roast Chicken with Stock pg 29, Chicken Broth pg 29, Chicken Vegetable Soup pg 31,
  Curry Chicken Salad pg 60

Chili Peppers

~ *Chipotle*
  Apricot Glazed Chops with Carrots pg 92
~ *Habanero*
  Red Rebel Soup pg 71, Black Bean, Corn and Avocado Salad pg 79, Pineapple Blueberry
  Slaw pg 94
~ *Jalapeno*
  Pico Di Gallo pg 52, Super Nachos and Tacos pg 66, Coconut Rice Salad with Cilantro-Lime
  Vinaigrette pg 80, Classic Chili pg 98, Vegetarian Chili pg 98
~ *Roasted Green*
  Chili N' Grits Breakfast Bake with Pico Di Gallo pg 52, Warm Cheese and Artichoke Dip pg 64

Chives

  Cultured Cream Cheese pg 25, Skillet Shrimp pg 39, Chili N Grits Breakfast Bake pg 52,
  Egg Salad and Endive pg 62, Asian Sesame Slaw pg 76

Cilantro (fresh)

  Chili N' Grits Breakfast Bake with Pico Di Gallo pg 52, Super Nachos and Tacos pg 66,
  Red Rebel Soup pg 71, Asian Sesame Slaw pg 76, Curry Roasted Cauliflower and
  Sweet Onion pg 78, Black Bean, Corn and Avocado Salad pg 79, Coconut Rice Salad with
  Cilantro-Lime Vinaigrette pg 80, Cilantro Lime Chicken pg 80, Pineapple Blueberry Slaw pg 94

Chocolate

~ *bittersweet*
  Honey Yogurt pg 24, Homemade Greek Yogurt pg 24, Super Snack Mix pg 65
~ *semisweet*
  Honey Yogurt pg 24, Homemade Greek Yogurt pg 24, Super Snack Mix pg 65, Chocolate Honey
  Nut Chippers pg 110, Fudgy Cream Frosting pg 111, Chocolate Raspberry Torte pg 118, Cocoa Nut
  Crust pg 118, Chocolate Ganache Glaze pg 118
~ *Cookies*
  Chocolate Cookie Crust pg 118

Cocoa Powder (unsweetened)

Coco-Nut Spread pg 7, Honey Yogurt pg 24, Homemade Greek Yogurt pg 24, Fruit Smoothies pg 56, Chocolate Honey Nut Chippers pg., Chocolate Raspberry Torte pg 118, Cocoa Nut Crust pg 118

Coconut

~ *flaked*

about pg 16, *toasted* pg 16

Overnight Oats pg 22, Honey Yogurt pg 24, Homemade Greek Yogurt pg 24, Coconut Lime Truffles pg 112, Lemon Coconut Truffles pg 112, Chocolate Raspberry Torte pg 118, Cocoa Nut Crust pg 118, Apricot Ricotta Cheesecake with Fruit pg 120, Macaroon Crust pg 120

~ *milk*

Overnight Oats pg 22, Scrambled Eggs pg 36, Berry and Cheese Crepes with Maple Spiced Nuts pg 50, Nut Butter and Jam Crepes pg 50, Fruit Smoothies pg 56, Harvest Bisque pg 72, Coconut Rice Salad with Cilantro-Lime Vinaigrette pg 80, Pecan Pumpkin Pie with Maple Whip pg 126, Pumpkin Pie pg 126

- *oil*

about pg 7

Coco-nut Spread pg 7, Cajun Rice pg 21, Popped Corn pg 58, Super Snack Mix pg 65, Red Rebel Soup pg 71, Harvest Bisque pg 72, Curry Roasted Cauliflower and Sweet Onion pg 78, Apricot Glazed Chops and Carrots pg 92, Yummy Yam Fries pg 95, Baked Banana Date and Nut Bread pg 113, Carrot Cakes with Cinnamon Cream Frosting pg 114, Zucchini Fudge Brownies pg 122

- *sugar,* refer to sugar pg 157

Corn

~ *flour*

Berry and Cheese Crepes with Maple-Spiced Nuts pg 50, Nut Butter and Jam Crepes pg 50, Figgy Puddin' with Vanilla Brandy Cream pg 128

~ *dried kernels*

Popped Corn pg 58

~ *fresh kernels*

Black Bean, Corn and Avocado Salad pg 79, Classic Chili pg 98, Vegetarian Chili pg 98

~ *meal (grits, polenta)*

Chili N Grits Breakfast Casserole with Pico Di Gallo pg 52, Polenta Lasagna pg 88, Vegetarian Polenta Lasagna pg 88

Cranberries (dried)

Overnight Oats pg 22, Honey Yogurt pg 24, Homemade Greek Yogurt pg 24, Super Snack Mix pg 65

Endive (Belgium)

   Egg Salad and Endive pg 62

Fennel (fresh)

   Grilled Orange Balsamic Chicken with Grapes pg 96, Maple Balsamic Root Salad pg 107

Feta Cheese

   Lemon Veggie Quinoa Salad pg 82, Everyday Italian Salad pg 89, Cauliflower Puttenesca pg 103, Eggplant Puttenesca pg 103

Fig

   Figgy Puddin' with Vanilla Brandy Cream pg 128

Fish

~ *mahi mahi*

   Grilled Mahi Mahi with Pineapple Blueberry Slaw pg 94

~ *salmon*

   Wild Balsamic Salmon pg 40, Balsamic Salmon with Berries Goat Cheese and Greens pg 40

~ *white (tilapia, haddock, halibut)*

   Broiled White Fish pg 38

Flour

~ *All purpose*

   about pg 8

   Sweet Crepes pg 50, Irish Stew and Irish Soda Bread pg 90, Chocolate Honey Nut Chippers pg 110, Zucchini Fudge Brownies pg 122, Apple Butternut Muffins pg 125

~ *Arrowroot;* refer to *Arrowroot* in Index

~ *Buckwheat;* refer to *Buckwheat* in Index

~ *Corn;* refer to *Corn* in Index

~ *Tapioca;* refer to *Tapioca* in Index

~ *Whole Grain Spelt and Whole Wheat Flour*

   about pg 8

   Sweet Crepes pg 50, Irish Soda Bread pg 91, Baked Banana Date and Nut Bread pg 113, Carrot Cakes pg 114, Blackberry Cheese Squares pg., Apple Butternut Muffins pg 125, Pumpkin Muffins pg 125

Garlic (fresh)

   Roasted Beef Bone Broth pg 27, Veggie Beef Soup pg 28, Classic Roast Chicken with Stock pg 29, Chicken Broth pg 29, Turkey Broth pg 29, Skillet Shrimp pg 39, Chili N. Grits Breakfast Casserole with Pico Di Gallo pg 52, Super Nachos and Tacos pg 66, Warm Cheese and Artichoke Dip pg 64, Veggie Minestrone pg 68, Asparagus Bisque pg 69, Tomato Soup Florentine pg 70, Red Rebel Soup pg 71, Lemon Veggie Quinoa Salad pg 82, Black Bean, Corn and Avocado Salad pg 79, Roasted Brussels Sprouts pg 85, Polenta Lasagna pg 88,

Honey (raw), continued

Pineapple Blueberry Slaw pg 94, Kale Pesto Rice pg 105, Chocolate Honey Nut Chippers pg 110., Almond Cream Frosting pg 111, Coconut Lime Truffles pg 112, Cinnamon Cream Frosting pg 115, Honey Cream Frosting pg 115, Honey Almond Whip pg 116, Apricot Ricotta Cheese Cake with Fruit pg 120, Blackberry Cheese Squares pg 124, Vanilla Brandy Cream pg 128

Hot Sauce

Chili N' Grits Breakfast Bake with Pico Di Gallo pg 52, Harvest Bisque pg 72, Homemade Chorizo pg 44

Jalapeño Chili; refer to *Chili Peppers* in the index

Jam/Organic Whole Fruit Preserves

Overnight Oats pg 22, Homemade Greek Yogurt pg 24, Crepes with Nut Butter and Jam pg 50, Fruit Smoothies pg 56, Asian Sesame Slaw pg 76, Apricot Glazed Chops and Carrots pg 92, Apricot Ricotta Cheesecake with Fruit pg 120, Blackberry Cheese Squares pg 124, Figgy Puddin' pg 128

Jicama

Grilled Mahi Mahi with Pineapple Blueberry Slaw pg 94

Kale

Poached Greens N' Eggs in Broth pg 27, Kale Chips pg 59, Kale Chopped Salad pg 84, Kale Pesto Rice pg 105

Kefir

about pg 23
Fruit Smoothies pg 56

Kohlrabi

Super Broccoli Salad pg 77

Lamb

Grilled or Broiled Chops pg 43, Irish Stew pg 90

Lemon

Chicken Vegetable Soup pg 31, Skillet Shrimp pg 39, Broiled White Fish pg 38, Chicken Tenders pg 41, Family Frittata pg 49, Berry and Cheese Crepes with Maple-Spiced Nuts pg 50, Warm Cheese and Artichoke Dip pg 64, Asparagus Bisque pg 69, Broccoli Cheddar Bisque pg 69, Lemon Veggie Quinoa Salad pg 82, Lemon Herb Dressing pg 82, Cauliflower Puttenesca pg 103, Eggplant Puttenesca pg 103, Strawberry Spinach Salad with Lemon Poppy Seed Vinaigrette pg 93, Kale Pesto Rice pg 105, Pecan Crusted Pork Tenderloin with Pear Cream pg 106, Lemon Coconut Truffles pg 112, Strawberry Lemon Almond Cream Cake pg 116

Lentils

about pg 16
Red Rebel Soup pg 71

Onions

~ *green (scallions)*
Cultured Cream Cheese Hors d'oeuvres pg 25, Chili N' Grits Breakfast Bake with Pico Di Gallo pg 52, Family Frittata pg 49, Curry Chicken Salad pg 60, Super Nachos and Tacos pg 66, Asian Sesame Slaw pg 76, Super Broccoli Salad pg 77, Lemon Veggie Quinoa Salad pg 82, Coconut Rice Salad with Cilantro-Lime vinaigrette pg 80, Everyday Italian Salad pg 89, Strawberry Spinach Salad with Lemon Poppy seed Vinaigrette pg 93, Classic Chili pg 98, Vegetarian Chili pg 98, Gram's Slow Roasted Country BBQ Ribs pg 100, Apple Cheddar salad with Maple vinaigrette pg 101

~ *red*
Pico Di Gallo pg 52, Super Nachos and Tacos pg 66, Lemon Veggie Quinoa Salad pg 82, Everyday Italian Salad pg 89, Classic Chili pg 98, Vegetarian Chili pg 98

~ *Sweet Vidalia*
BEST Salad pg 54, Pico Di Gallo pg 52, Super Naches and Tacos pg 66, Super broccoli Salad pg 77, Lemon Veggie Quinoa Salad pg 82, Curry Roasted Cauliflower with Sweet Onion pg 78, Kale Chopped Salad pg 84, Everyday Italian Salad pg 89, Apple Cheddar Salad with Maple Vinaigrette pg 101, Classic Chili pg 98, Vegetarian Chili pg 98

~ *Yellow*
Cajun Rice pg 21, Roasted Beef Bone Broth pg 27, Poached Greens N' Eggs in Broth pg 27, Classic Roast Chicken pg 29, Chicken Broth pg 29, Turkey Broth pg 29, Chicken Vegetable Soup pg 31, BEST Salad pg 54, Family Frittata pg 49, Breakfast Casserole pg 49, Chili N Grits Breakfast Bake with Pico Di Gallo pg 52, Veggie Minestrone pg 68, Asparagus Bisque pg 69, Broccoli Cheddar Bisque pg 69, Tomato Soup Florentine pg 70, Red Rebel Soup pg 71, Harvest Bisque pg 72, Super Nachos and Tacos pg 66, Super broccoli Salad pg 77, Lemon Veggie Quinoa Salad pg 82, Everyday Italian Salad pg 89, Cauliflower Puttenesca pg 103, Eggplant Puttenesca pg 103, Irish Stew pg 90, Meatballs and Marinara pg 104, Apple Cheddar Salad with Maple Vinaigrette pg 101, Crispy Tater Chips and Onion pg 101, Classic Chili pg 98, Vegetarian Chili pg 98, Pecan Crusted Pork Tenderloin with Pear Cream pg 106, Maple Balsamic Root Salad pg 107

Orange

~ *mandarin*
Asian Sesame Slaw pg 76, Pineapple Blueberry Slaw pg 94, Apricot Ricotta Cheesecake with Fruit pg 120

~ *juice*
Yummy Yam Fries pg 95, Grilled Orange Balsamic Chicken with Grapes pg 96

~ *liquor*
about pg 10
Fresh Fruit with Marscapone Dip pg 61, Strawberry Lemon Almond Cream Cake pg 116

Oregano

Veggie Minestrone pg 68, Everyday Italian Salad pg 89, Cauliflower Puttenesca pg 103, Eggplant Puttenesca pg 103, Meatballs and Marinara pg 104, Classic Chili pg 98, Vegetarian Chili pg 98

Pasta

Chicken Vegetable Soup pg 31, Kale Pesto pg 105

Papaya

Fruit Smoothies pg 56, Fresh Fruit with Marscapone Dip pg 61

Parmesan Cheese

Veggie Beef Soup pg 28, Poached Greens N' Eggs in Broth pg 27, Chicken Vegetable Soup pg 31, Broiled White Fish pg 38, Skillet Shrimp pg 39, Family Frittata pg 49, Breakfast Casserole pg 49, Warm Cheese and Artichoke Dip pg 64, Veggie Minestrone pg 68, Asparagus Bisque pg 69, Tomato Soup Florentine pg 70, Lemon Veggie Quinoa Salad pg 82, Polenta Lasagna with Every day Italian Salad pg 88, Vegetarian Polenta Lasagna pg 88, Cauliflower Puttenesca pg 103, Eggplant Puttenesca pg 103, Meatballs N Marinara with Kale Pesto Rice pg 104

Parsley (fresh)

Cultured Cream Cheese (Hors d'oeuvres) pg 25, Roasted Beef Bone Broth pg 27, Veggie Beef Soup pg 28, Poached Greens N' Eggs in Broth pg 27, Classic Roast Chicken with Stock pg 29, Chicken Broth pg 29, Turkey Broth pg 29, Chicken Vegetable Soup pg 31, Skillet Shrimp pg 39, Veggie Minestrone pg 68, Asparagus Bisque pg 69, Broccoli Cheddar Bisque pg 69, Tomato Soup Florentine pg 70, Lemon Veggie Quinoa Salad pg 82, Lemon Herb Dressing pg 82, Polenta Lasagna pg 88, Vegetarian Polenta Lasagna pg 88, Cauliflower Puttenesca pg 103, Eggplant Puttenesca pg 103, Irish Stew pg 90, Gram's Slow Roasted Country BBQ Ribs pg 100, Pulled Pork Sandwiches pg 100, Meatballs and Marinara with Kale Pesto Rice pg 104, Pecan Crusted Pork Tenderloin with Pear Cream pg 106

Parsnips

Chicken Broth pg 29, Chicken Vegetable Soup pg 31, Veggie Beef Soup pg 28, Poached Greens N' Eggs in Broth pg 27

Peaches

Fruit Smoothies pg 56, Fresh Fruit with Mascarpone Dip pg 61, Apricot Ricotta Cheesecake with Fruit pg 120, Fruit Crisp pg 123

Peanut Butter

Nut Butter and Jam Crepes pg 50, Fruit Smoothies pg 56, Chocolate Honey Nut Chippers pg 110

Pear

Honey Yogurt pg 24, Homemade Greek Yogurt pg 24, Pecan Crusted Pork Tenderloin with Pear Cream pg 106, Fruit Crisp pg 123

Peas

Chicken Vegetable Soup pg 31, Kale Pesto Rice pg 105

Potatoes

Classic Roast Chicken with Gravy and Mashed Potatoes pg 29, Asparagus Bisque pg 69, Broccoli Cheddar Bisque pg 69, Rosemary Roasted Potatoes pg 97, Crispy Tater Chips and Onions pg 101

Provolone Cheese

Lemon Veggie Quinoa Salad pg 82, Everyday Italian Salad pg 89

Pumpkin

Harvest Bisque pg 72, Apple Pumpkin Muffins pg 125, Pecan Pumpkin Pie pg 126, Pumpkin Pie pg 126

Pumpkin Seeds

Harvest Bisque pg 72, Curry Roasted Cauliflower and Sweet Onion pg 78, Yummy Yam Fries pg 95

Quinoa

Red Rebel Soup pg 71, Lemon Veggie Quinoa Salad pg 82

Raisins

Overnight Oats pg 22, Homemade Greek Yogurt pg 24, Honey Yogurt pg 24, Curry Chicken Salad pg 60, Great Granola pg 63, Super Snack Mix pg 65, Carrot Cakes with Cinnamon Cream Frosting pg 114

Raspberries

Honey Yogurt pg 24, Homemade Greek Yogurt pg 24, Balsamic Salmon with Berries Goat Cheese and Green pg 40, Berry and Cheese Crepes with Maple-Spiced Nuts pg 50, Fruit Smoothies pg 56, Fresh Fruit with Mascarpone Dip pg 61, Chocolate Raspberry Torte pg 118, Apricot Ricotta Cheesecake with Fruit pg 120

Rice

~ *brown- long grain and short*

basic soaking and cooking pg 14, Cajun Rice pg 21, Chicken and Vegetable Soup pg 31, Kale Pesto Rice pg 105

~ *wild*

basic soaking and cooking instructions pg 14, Chicken and Vegetable Soup pg 31

Ricotta Cheese

Polenta Lasagna pg 88, Vegetarian Polenta Lasagna pg 88, Apricot Ricotta Cheesecake with Fruit pg 120

Romano Cheese

Veggie Beef Soup pg 28, Poached Greens N' Eggs in Broth pg 27, Chicken Vegetable Soup pg 31, Family Frittata pg 49, Breakfast Casserole pg 49, Warm Cheese and Artichoke Dip pg 64, Veggie Minestrone pg 68, Asparagus Bisque pg 69, Tomato Soup Florentine pg 70, Lemon Veggie Quinoa Salad pg 82, Cauliflower Puttenesca pg 103, Eggplant Puttenesca pg 103, Meatballs and Marinara with Kale Pesto Rice pg 104, Grilled Orange Balsamic Chicken with Grapes and Rosemary Roasted Potatoes pg 96

Rosemary

Classic Roast Chicken with Stock pg 29, Chicken Broth pg 29, Grilled Orange Balsamic Chicken with Grapes and Rosemary Roasted Potatoes pg 96, Maple Balsamic Root Salad pg 107

Sage

Classic Roast Chicken with Stock pg 29, Chicken Broth pg 29

Salsa; refer to *Tomatoes*

Sausage

~ *Breakfast*
Prepared Eggs pg 36, Baked Breakfast Sausage pg 37, Berry and Cheese Crepes with Maple Spiced Nuts pg 50, Chili N' Grits Breakfast Bake with Pico Di Gallo pg 52

~ *Chorizo*
Prepared Eggs pg 36, Homemade Chorizo pg 44, Chili N' Grits Breakfast Bake with Pico Di Gallo pg 52, Super Nachos and Tacos pg 66

~ *Italian*
Polenta Lasagna pg 88

Scallion; refer to *Green Onion*

Sesame Oil

Asian Sesame Slaw pg 76

Sesame Seeds

Asian Sesame Slaw pg 76, Sesame Tandoori Chicken with Honey pg 102

Shallot

Roasted Brussels Sprouts pg 85, Apple Cheddar Salad with Maple Vinaigrette pg 101, Pecan Crusted Pork Tenderloin with Maple Balsamic Root Salad pg 107

Sour Cream

BEST Salad pg 54, Chili N' Grits Breakfast Casserole with Pico Di Gallo pg 52, Super Nachos and Tacos pg 66, Asparagus Bisque pg 69, Broccoli Cheddar Bisque pg 69, Tomato Soup Florentine pg 70, Harvest Bisque pg 72, Super Broccoli Salad pg 77, Kale Chopped Salad pg 84, Strawberry Spinach Salad with Lemon Poppy seed Vinaigrette pg 93, Pineapple Blueberry Slaw pg 94, Classic Chili pg 98, Vegetarian Chili pg 98, Meatballs and Marinara pg 104, Pecan Crusted Pork Tenderloin pg 106, Fudgy Cream Frosting pg 111,

Sour Cream, continued
   Baked Banana Date and Nut Bread pg 113, Carrot Cakes with Cinnamon Cream Frosting pg 114, Fruit Crisp pg 123

Sour Kraut
   about pg 23, Irish Stew pg 90

Soy Sauce (Tamari)
   about pg 8, Winter Squash Cups pg 98

Spaghetti Squash
   Winter Squash Cups pg 98, Meatballs and Marinara pg 104

Spelt Flour; See *Flour*

Spirulina Powder; *about* pg 8

Spinach
~ *fresh*
   Poached Greens N' Eggs in Broth pg 27, Chicken Vegetable Soup pg 31, Skillet Shrimp pg 39, BEST Salad pg 54, Tomato Soup Florentine pg 70, Curry Roasted Cauliflower and Sweet Onion pg 78, Lemon Veggie Quinoa Salad pg 82, Coconut Rice Salad with Cilantro-Lime Vinaigrette pg 80, Strawberry Spinach Salad with Lemon Poppy seed Vinaigrette pg 93, Apple Cheddar Salad with maple Vinaigrette pg 101, Grilled Orange Balsamic Chicken with Grapes and Roasted Rosemary Potatoes pg 96, Maple Balsamic Root Salad pg 107
~ *frozen*
   Fruit Smoothies pg 56, Warm Cheese and Artichoke Dip pg 64, Polenta Lasagna pg 88, Vegetarian Polenta Lasagna pg 88

Strawberries
   about pg 8
   Honey Yogurt pg 24, Homemade Greek Yogurt pg 24, Balsamic Salmon with Berries and Goat Cheese pg 40, Berry and Cheese Crepes with Maple-Spiced Nuts pg 50, Fruit Smoothies pg 56, Fresh Fruit with Mascarpone Dip pg 61, Strawberry Spinach Salad with Lemon Poppy seed Vinaigrette pg 93, Apricot Ricotta Cheesecake with Fruit pg 120

Sugar
   about pg 9
   Baked Banana Date and Nut Bread pg 113, Carrot Cakes with Cinnamon Cream Frosting pg 114, Apple Butternut Muffins pg 125, Apple Pumpkin Muffins pg 125
~ *coconut*
   Carrot Cakes pg 114, Zucchini Fudge Brownies pg. 122, Fruit Crisp pg 123, Apple Butternut Muffins pg 125, Apple Pumpkin Muffins pg 125 ~natural brown (sucanat or coconut)

Sugar, continued

~ *pure cane*
  about pg 8
  Berry and Cheese Crepes with Maple-Spiced Nuts pg 50, Strawberry Lemon Almond Cream Cake pg 116, Chocolate Raspberry Torte pg 118, Zucchini Fudge Brownies pg 122, Fruit Crisp pg 123, Blackberry Cheese Squares pg 124, Apple Butternut Muffins pg 125, Apple Pumpkin Muffins pg 125, Pecan Pumpkin Pie with Maple Whip pg 126, Pumpkin Pie pg 126

~ *turbinado*
  about pg 8
  Berry and Cheese Crepes with Maple-Spiced Nuts pg 50, Strawberry Lemon Almond Cream cake pg 116, Chocolate Raspberry Torte pg 118, Zucchini Fudge Brownies pg 122, Fruit Crisp pg 123, Blackberry Cheese Squares pg 124, Apple Butternut Muffins pg 125, Apple Pumpkin Muffins pg 125

Sunflower

~ *Seeds*
  Super-Toasty Nuts and Seeds pg 15, Toasted Nuts and Seeds pg 16, Honey Yogurt pg 24, Homemade Greek Yogurt pg 24, Super Snack Mix pg 65, Super Broccoli Salad pg 77

~ *Butter*
  Coco-nut Spread pg 7, Nut Butter and Jam Crepes pg 50, Fruit Smoothies pg 56

Sweet Potato; see *yam*

Tahini
  Coco-nut Spread pg 7, Veggie Minestrone pg 68

Tapioca Flour
  about pg. 8
  Berry and Cheese Crepes pg 50, Irish Stew pg 90, Chocolate Honey Nut Chippers pg 110, Zucchini Fudge Brownies pg 122, Figgy Puddin' pg 128

Thyme
  Classic Roast Chicken with Stock pg 29, Harvest Bisque pg 72, Lemon Veggie Quinoa Salad pg 82, Lemon and Herb Dressing pg 82, Maple Balsamic Root Salad pg 107

Tomatoes

~ *crushed (canned)*
  Tomato Soup Florentine pg 70, Meatballs and Marinara pg 104, Classic Chili pg 98, Vegetarian Chili pg 98

~ *diced (canned)*
  Veggie Beef Soup pg 28, Poached Greens N' Eggs in Broth pg 27, Veggie Minestrone pg 68, Classic Chili pg 98, Vegetarian Chili pg 98

Tomatoes, continued

~ *fresh*

Prepared Eggs pg 36, Baked Bacon pg 37, Skillet Shrimp pg 39, BEST Salad pg 54, Family Frittata pg 49, Breakfast Casserole pg 49, Pico Di Gallo pg 52, Warm Artichoke Dip pg 64, Super Nachos and Tacos pg 66, Lemon Veggie Quinoa Salad pg 82, Everyday Italian Salad pg 89, Kale Pesto Rice pg 105

~ *paste*

Veggie Minestrone pg 68, Irish Stew pg 90

~ *salsa (prepared in jar)*

Super Nachos and Tacos pg 66, Classic Chili pg 98, Vegetarian Chili pg 98

~ *sauce*

Polenta Lasagna pg 88, Vegetarian Polenta Lasagna pg 88, Meatballs and Marinara pg 104

Turkey

~ *carcass*

Turkey Broth pg 29

~ *ground*

Homemade Chorizo pg 44

Venison

Irish Stew pg 90

Vinegar; refer to *Apple Cider Vinegar*, and *Balsamic Vinegar*

Walnuts

Super-Toasty Nuts and Seeds pg 15, Toasted Nuts and Seeds pg 16, Overnight Oats pg 22, Honey Yogurt pg 24, Homemade Greek Yogurt pg 24, Great Granola pg 63, Super Snack Mix pg 65, Berry and Cheese Crepes with Maple-Spiced Nuts pg 50, Kale Pesto Rice pg 105, Apple Cheddar Salad with Maple Vinaigrette pg 101, Baked Banana Date and Nut Bread pg 113, Coconut Lime Truffles pg 112, Lemon Coconut Truffles pg 112, Fruit Crisp pg 123, Black Berry Cheese Squares pg 124, Apple Butternut Muffins pg 125, Apple Pumpkin Muffins pg 125

Whole Wheat Flour; refer to *Flour*

Wine

~ *red*

about pg. 8

Irish Stew pg 90

~ *white*

about pg. 8

Roasted Beef Bone Broth pg 27, Veggie N' Beef Soup pg 27, Chicken Broth pg 29, Asparagus Bisque pg 69, Broccoli Cheddar Bisque pg 69

Whey

Yam

Yogurt (plain whole milk)

Zucchini